I0828326

PEOPLE OF THE FLINT HILLS

PEOPLE OF THE FLINT HILLS

BLUESTEM PASTURE PORTRAITS

JOHN E. BROWN

Published by The History Press
Charleston, SC 29403
www.historypress.net

Front cover photography courtesy of the Sylvester family of rural Wamego, Kansas.

First published 2014

ISBN 978-1-5402-1184-2

Library of Congress CIP data applied for.

Notice: The information in this book is true and complete to the best of our knowledge. It is offered without guarantee on the part of the author or The History Press. The author and The History Press disclaim all liability in connection with the use of this book.

To Lee Ann, who made everything better

CONTENTS

Contents

ACKNOWLEDGEMENTS

I am particularly grateful for the assistance of Ms. Susan Adams of the Flint Hills Discovery Center for her introduction to families from her region of the hills. The reader will find no more affecting, more knowledgeable accounting of the Flint Hills than in the displays and programs there in the architectural gem at the river's edge in downtown Manhattan. Also, Mr. Mike Beam of the Kansas Livestock Association directed me to stories that illuminate the book cover to cover. Thanks, buddy.

All the photographs in the book are the author's, with these exceptions.

The photograph of the young buckaroo on page 26 appears through the courtesy of Mike and Rene Wiggins of rural Eureka, Kansas.

The photographs on pages 13, 40, 43 (top) and 123 are the beautiful work of Ms. Alisha Gibb of Strong City, Kansas. More of Alisha's photography may be seen on her blog crazycowboywife.wordpress.com.

INTRODUCTION

The Flint Hills lope across eighty-two thousand square miles of Kansas from Marshall and Washington Counties in the north, Shawnee County in the east, Geary County on their western edge and on down into Chautauqua County, Kansas, and Kay County, Oklahoma, on the south. The Flint Hills represent the largest and one of the last stands of the tallgrass prairie in North America. The Nature Conservancy reports that the tallgrass prairie ecosystem is the most radically changed major habitat type in the country with more acres lost than in any other American ecosystem. Only about 4 percent of the great grasslands remain, and the Flint Hills constitute 70 percent of the surviving tallgrass prairie.

I live in the rock-bottomed heart of the Kansas Flint Hills, the most compelling expanse of bluestem prairie in the world, pastures that stretch to a child's notion of infinity, protein-rich grass jitterbugging thigh deep in the random whirls of a freshening wind. Above this ranch bends a sky that can't stop itself from deepening, from expanding, from by turns lowering and brightening with colors that come from heaven's waiting room. And not a single, solitary intrusion of the twenty-first century in sight.

These hills encourage the best in all of us: humility, contentment, resolve, a quiet focus far beyond the self. They bring a welcome sort of separation. A good lonesome.

The people who live here have learned the demands of distance. The citizens of the smallest towns, the ranchers and farmers of the Flint Hills, have learned self-reliance because the nearest grocery store lies thirty miles away, the closest pediatrician practices seventy miles away, the last picture show closed fifteen years ago. And because the nearest

NEBRASKA
MISSOURI
KANSAS
Missouri
Kansas
Manhattan
KONZA PRAIRIE PRESERVE
Junction City
Alma
Eskridge
Topeka
Lawrence
Kansas City
Alta Vista
Council Grove
TALLGRASS PRAIRIE NATIONAL PRESERVE
Emporia
Strong City
Cottonwood Falls
Florence
Cedar Point
Bazaar
Matfield Green
Cassoday
Arkansas
El Dorado
Eureka
Wichita
FLINT HILLS TALLGRASS PRAIRIE ECO-REGION
Sedan
FLINT HILLS
0mi
50
0km
50
OKLAHOMA

neighbor lives but three miles away, the people of the Flint Hills have learned the value of shared everything, labor most of all.

For all of their rugged independence, the families of the Flint Hills are facing new economic threats these days, gone now the easy choices to live where their great-grandparents lived, to care for cattle horseback on ranches handed down, generation after generation looking to live their lives way out in the open. The great-great-great-grandchildren of Kansas homesteaders must find these days other ways to make a living. So off they go into such jobs as they can find in the city or to some cottage industry (saddle-making, agritourism, leatherwork, haying, carpentry, firewood delivered to a suburban rack) or on into geographically distant work where the skills of the cowman (observation, persistence, determination and raw muscle on the one hand and welding, construction and mechanics on the other) command a livable wage.

This great wide country cannot escape economic realities generated by the irresistible forces of supply and demand but, just as much, by a government gone all out of control in its regulation of the air we breathe, the water we drink. These days, all of us in rural America must live by rules made almost entirely by bureaucrats who haven't a clue to the mysteries of lives predicated on both self-reliance and concern for one's neighbor. The fools who write this nation's laws today know not "neighbor" as a noun. They cannot possibly understand the implications of the word as a verb.

These are stories of people descended from women and men of grit and bone, of steeled resolve, living in the wrap and the immediacy of these cloudless distances, in places where you need no compass to find your way home.

When you can see forever, you can always find a place to make a stand.

PART I
LOOKING BACK: THE OLD SCHOOL

Albert Pickell

You could always tell when Albert Pickell had made a major point. He'd up the intensity factor on the eye contact, and he'd give a straight, hard up-and-down wag of his head accompanied by a small "yep," sometimes a jab of the finger and always a cackle from somewhere out by an open gate. At that moment, he was as engaging a cowboy as you might ever want to know. And the truth of what he had just said stood biblical, beyond discussion.

Albert Pickell did not boast, and so you believed him when he said that no man had ever beaten him in the contest of hand-and-forearm strength known as "Twist the Broom Handle," his credibility supported by the fifteen hundred some feet of hand-braided halters, girts and cinches hanging on the wall behind him.

Marie Pickell, who married Albert fifty-five years before she gave up on him and died, did not boast when she told the story of the yearling bull who would, on call, walk to a fence and drink from a Styrofoam cup in Albert's hand—this being the very same bull who, a few months later, contrary to Albert's instructions, was taken out of a bunch of cows at the local sale barn and, in protest, broke down the pens and every gate standing between him and Albert some three miles away.

Albert always rode big, stout horses, most of which he bought and broke as colts. Even before he commenced to cowboying at the age of fifteen, he had spent years in the company of Percherons, the teams he fed and harnessed every morning of his childhood. His family farmed oats, corn and wheat, and the Pickells used mules and draft horses to plow the black dirt of rural Elk Falls, Kansas.

In the best ranch job he ever had, Albert would stop and feed the horses on his way to work early, early in the morning. In a testament to the liberality of his Percheron ways, he found no contradiction between "the best ranch job I ever had" and the manager's rule that the cowboys on that ranch punch a time clock. When the foreman discovered that Albert was feeding the horses before he punched in, Mr. Pickell was ordered to go to the barn, register on the clock and drive back to the corral in a company truck with his sweet mix. "Some of those other hands resented the time clock," he remembered, "but I liked it. I made an extra seventy-five dollars a month by the owner's knowing just how much time I was putting in."

He worked on the big southeast Kansas ranches: the old Sutton with the time clock; the McKinney near Howard; the J Bar J east of Fall River, at the time the largest commercial Angus operation in the state, with four thousand mother cows scattered among the woolliest, jack-oak country that the Sunflower State has to offer. On the J Bar, in 1960, with the worst, wettest late-winter snowstorm in memory underfoot, the ranch's principal feed truck—a cab-over Jeep—spun itself up to the axles. Albert went down south, bought a team of mules from his dad and commenced to feed cattle the hard way. He started with a rubber-tired trailer, but by the end of the first week, he had changed out to wooden wheels with three-inch iron rims, also purchased from his father. By the end of the six weeks of mud and cold, he was completing the eleven-mile feed route in just an hour longer than he had ever done it with the Jeep.

On the McKinney ranch, tractors had replaced teams early on, and one day, the International came over on top of him on fire. His boot stuck, he was unable to get clear and the left wheel crushed his ribs. He counted the bumps in the road to a hospital fifty-some miles away. The orderlies there refused to allow him to walk up the steps to the hospital door. They ordered him onto a cart, and then, undermanned, they bounced and jostled him halfway up the stairs until they found extra help. Turns out, the help was drunk, and they dumped Albert just outside the elevator, where they proceeded to slam his head in the door. He was taken to an emergency room where an inexperienced nurse taped his ribs so tight they buckled. The tractor didn't kill him, but small-town healthcare damned near did, and he could thereafter grab at his shirt and produce an outgrowth of bone that did not really belong in that part of a cowboy's anatomy.

The cowboy's quintessential task: ride the pastures, find the sick ones and doctor them. Always has been. Always will be.

Albert Pickell took care of cattle well into his eighties, one thousand head per summer, although in the last few seasons, he left his rope in the barn when he and old Kid, himself almost an octogenarian in a well-spent equine lifetime, went out to pen some. Albert at last accepted a four-wheeler to feed mineral and check fence.

To the very end, he made his tack; Marie died and Albert shoved off to a brand-new old-folks home with matronly wallpaper everywhere amid a general burgundy and green color scheme that sort of matched his skin where the bone stuck through. Consumer orders for his intricate, unbreakable weaves rolled in from Oregon to Texas, some hands refusing to rope a big steer unless an Albert Pickell girt looped under the fenders. His inventions—an easily adjustable bridle, a quick-release halter for cattle and impossibly soft, impossibly strong reins made from reworked, worn-out lariats—remained his most popular products along with the saddle pockets he crafted from the tops of old boots. The day before he died, he made a twenty-year girt in less than an hour.

Some days, I'd go to see him in the home, and we'd sit, and he'd tell his stories of horses and cattle, and he'd drink a Diet Dr. Pepper or two. Some days we'd ride out south and drink beer at pasture gates he'd built half a century ago.

An orange-and-white pigging string hangs from the mirror in my feed truck, just like five others given to the pallbearers at his funeral. When we carried him out to the plot next to Marie, I felt a little poke in my chest. As the ground came up to eat him—damned if I didn't hear it—a cackle in the wind over east there, off toward the J Bar J, the world lonesome now. Empty for sure.

Because God was busy at the moment, Himself laughing, a divine vein or two bulging in the toughest game of Twist the Broom Handle He had ever, ever known.

Kathryn Jackson

The assistants at the glamour photography studio lacked wherewithal. By their own admission, nothing among their rack of gowns and stacks of costume jewelry seemed exactly right for this particular customer. At eighty-six years of age, ranch woman Kathryn Jackson had come to town for a fancy portrait. Finally, customer and studio settled on a blue-sequined number, long black gloves and four-inch dangly rhinestone earrings to go with the upswept hair and the extra makeup. The picture was made, and Kathryn proudly took it home to her Happy, and he said to her, "That's nice, Kathryn. Who is it?"

Before the stroke, Hap Jackson had been a cowboy's cowboy, riding his first pasture at the age of four, living all his life on ranches he worked and then, at last, owned in western Greenwood County, Kansas. To his dying day, he accused Kathryn of "chasing him," of corralling him into marriage to the new schoolteacher who lived with his folks during her first year in public education. They eloped to Marion, fifty miles away, during haying season, and they came home and told no one outside of family of their union. (In those days, the teaching jobs went first to married men, last of all to married women, and the newlyweds needed Kathryn's income, eighty-five dollars a month teaching at Little Sallyards School, "a fabulous salary back then," per the glamour queen.) In her heart, the young bride knew that the first trip would be the last of an anniversary nature: Hap simply would not leave the ranch when it was time to hay.

In time, Kathryn began to write to children in the cities, sending them descriptions of seasonal work among the cattle and the cultivation. She

The school where Kathryn Jackson taught still stands across from the ranch house where she and Hap hid their marriage for an entire year.

cut pictures from *Farm Journal* to photograph her words. Most of all, she waited for a schoolchild of her and Happy's own, and after seventeen years of marriage, they had waited and prayed enough. Here came little Kathy and then, three years later, Harold Edmund, both joy-filled adoptions. Three years after Ed, at Christmas, Kathryn believed that she had developed a tumor. Unwilling to ruin the festivities, she waited until after the holidays to go to her doctor, who told her, "Kathryn, that's not a tumor." Margie made three, and the world of the Jackson ranch was perfect. Fecund, teeming with grass and calves and now children of her and Hap's own, the ranch stood ready for some visitors.

They came for years, these city kids, to fish and wade in the creek and milk a cow and find some fossils and pick some berries and play, of course, in the hay. Here they would come—three hundred in a spring—with adults trailing along behind the school buses to share in the fun. In one of life's eventual ironies, old Hap had—in time—to come from town himself, out to the ranch from the care home, to hear again the squeals and the giggles of children who found in his life's work the stuff of wonder. Kathryn built a ramp onto the front porch for her husband's wheelchair during those blessed years when he came home for a few hours. She pulled her little red wagon loaded with wood up the ramp, warming the house for his return. Until the very end, the department of motor vehicles recognized her visual, muscular and mental acuity, and she drove every day to be with him, to sit for a time with the man she ran to earth so long ago.

They're both gone now, Hap Jackson and his wife of eight decades.

But the neighbors, they still see her on the porch, rocking there, waiting for her husband, laughing in those stupid rhinestone earrings, knowing that she had done all she set out to do.

WALTER TALKINGTON

In Cottonwood Falls, Kansas, Walter Talkington has come downtown this afternoon. Walter is going to the post office. He pauses in front of the bank, sits for seven or eight minutes on the bench there in the shade, a time in which five women pass by, aged nineteen maybe to sixty-plus. Each one speaks. "Hi, Walt." "How are you today, sweetie?" "Pretty day, huh, Walter?" "Afternoon, Walt." "Hello, Mr. Talkington." And then he and his stick shuffle on down the sidewalk.

In the meantime, he has let it be known that his life has been a good one, that at age eighty-six, he has lived in but two houses, "one on each side of the high school. Now that's not getting around much in eighty-some years, is it?" He speaks of his semester at K-State, a degree in electrical engineering his plan. "Just hated it up there. One teacher begged me to stay," but he came home and went to work for the State of Kansas as a highway engineer. He allows as how he has run some mighty fine cows, his herd out on the thousand acres of grass he once owned. "I'm not a cowboy, but I sure know how to take care of cattle," he says. He has been a farmer most of all, an agribusinessman of the family-knows-best school in a Talkington partnership that involved his mother (Edith) and his brother (Dutch) as well. "We farmed two thousand acres," he says, the Talkingtons' cultivation matter of fact in its reach "from Peabody to east of Emporia, in corn and wheat and soybeans, with some alfalfa too." At the age of eighty-five, Edith Talkington was still driving the partnership's eight-wheel, articulated, 470-horsepower Steiger tractor.

He took time off to go to Hawaii, five trips across the Pacific all told. He "tried that beer-drinking, but it don't work." He signed up for dancing

Walter Talkington, en route.

RESERVED
Prairie PastTimes
Antiques & Crafts
OPEN

lessons in Fort Worth and became so proficient in the rhythmic movement of his farmer's feet that a terpsichorean outfit in Wichita hired him to be a promotional dancer in its traveling exhibitions. He favored the tango. Walter cackles. "I like that body-to-body stuff."

He did not marry, he says, "until I was forty-three years of age. And she just about broke me." He outlines the breakage: the new wife arriving with a huge hospital bill but, per her assurances, with an insurance policy to cover it. That first financial crisis overcome, Walter and Bernadean have lived happily on Plum Street for forty years. But hold on here.

Mr. Walter Talkington has turned to his own history of illness and injury. A baler broke both his arms in 1956, Walter trying to fix the infernal broken thing, trapping him in the chute. When help came, he gave instruction on how to tear down the baler, how to set him free. He has found mercy in the speed with which his troubles arrived. "All of my accidents have happened under twenty miles an hour," he announces with particular gratitude for the velocity of the freight train that demolished his pickup but allowed him to walk away unscathed.

Mr. Walter Talkington—slow to marry but quick to court—did in fact crisscross the state of Kansas in pursuit of the fair sex. He claims, with a lady friend waiting at Boot Hill, to have driven from Cottonwood Falls to Dodge City in two hours, a distance of 206 miles with, per Google Maps calculations, a driving time of three hours and twenty minutes along U.S. Highway 50 fraught with its superabundance of eighteen-wheelers. "I was going to see a school teacher," he reports, his friend's occupation somehow an offset to his driving habits.

The years gathered together, and no longer a farmer, the cow herd dispersed, he went to day labor for Wayne Rogler. The ranch headquarters stood thirteen miles south, an operation once encompassing some sixty thousand acres, including leased ground on which some fifteen thousand head of cattle were managed, with Walter haying in the summer, feeding cows in the winter. For twenty years, Walter made that drive down Highway 177.

And so it all has come round to this: his prop carved from a sumac bush, the old gentleman finding "those fancy sticks" all too heavy, Walter Talkington, beloved of women, walks to mail a letter, living large here in the last of the good old days.

Albert Wiggins

Albert Wiggins's speech split right down the middle. One minute he'd be telling stories of the old days with the asymmetric detail of a lifelong cowboy; the next he'd sound like a professor of something or other. He'd mention "heterosis factor" and "Warner-Braxler shear-force scale" with logical nonchalance and right reason, rare vocabulary all right, coming from a man who once sharpened hedge posts for fifty cents a day. Thirteen years old at the time, using an ax and a stump, he put a point on load after load of hedge, all winter long, making posts small enough to be driven down between the rocks but strong enough to hold the wire, posts—per Albert—"the size of pencils now, but they're still standing," Albert not being scientific at that moment, you understand.

His first horseback job came on the Culver Ranch in northern Greenwood County, Kansas. Albert bought cattle from the railheads at Cassoday and Matfield Green on drives that stretched across the hills for two dozen miles and more. "We'd unload cattle at night until the stockyards were full and then move out at daylight, while the rest of the crew unloaded the remainder of the train. A cowboy at the head of the drive could be home in bed before the last of the cattle left Cassoday."

One year, Mr. Culver brought three hundred bulls belonging to the United States military up out of Mexico, and he put young Albert in charge. When Albert gathered those pent-up, fence-busting bulls at summer's end, he discovered he didn't have a friend left in the cow-calf business. Then a government man in a black Lincoln pulled into the headquarters to announce that he wanted to count those bulls, one by one, as Albert and the boys drove them through a gate. "We tried it three or four times, and the sumbitch would lose count, and he'd make us do it again." When at last the government man allowed that he had his count, he brought out "the biggest chain with the biggest padlock I have ever seen, and he put them on that three-wire gate with a special seal attached. That was my first impression of those dumb government bastards, and it hasn't changed much since."

He has changed his mind about genetics several times.

"I've noticed that packers will pay a premium for an animal nobody has," he says, and such thinking has led to a lifetime of experimentation and testing and thinking some more. Albert's father gave him seven Shorthorn-cross heifers on his graduation from high school, and he has never been without a cow in the meantime—Shorthorns bred to Angus, Shorthorns to Herefords and their offspring back to Angus, black baldy replacement heifers bred to Santa Gertrudis and Charolais and, for the longest time now, Brangus to Brangus.

He was involved in carefully controlled tests of carcass traits on steers out of artificially inseminated Brangus cows. The participants in the test? Kansas State University, Texas A&M University, Auburn University and Albert Wiggins—he of the pink cowboy boots.

Back to the Mexican bulls: on that long-ago day when the load of five hundred shipped out of Madison, seventeen miles away, Mr. Culver told Albert to follow the drive and fix the fences the bulls would most surely damage, on a morning when the buckaroo Wiggins was wearing an inexpensive pair of new cowboy boots with fancy red inlaid uppers. It rained all day, and Albert fixed fences in the downpour. At day's end, five miles behind the drive, he looked down to see the cardboard inlays from his discount boots lying light, light red in the mud.

I loved Albert.

He wrote poems, variants on an unvarying theme: "John Brown is an ass." His rhyme scheme ("class," "glass," "sass," "bass") and slant rhymes ("vast," "mast," even the occasional archaic "hast") limited his range some, but it slowed him none, an insulting little ditty every other day or so waiting in my mailbox. One Sunday afternoon, the phone rang in my ranch office: Albert wondering if I'd ever heard of such a thing as a rhyming dictionary. He glowed when I showed up at his door with the book in my hand. Two weeks later came proof he'd been rhyming his eighty-year-old ass off.

The locals loved to dink good naturedly with the owners of the cattle who summered on our Flint Hills Kansas grass, what with gates cinched drum tight and, most of all, with proffered horses for the roundup, prize boobs ready to blow up at one itchy move. Albert documented the trickery in a stanza from a poem of some hundred lines about the gentle Wes James, his big Texas steers coming every summer to fatten with Albert's family, the influence of the rhyming dictionary obvious and then some.

We put Wes on Paco,
And Paco came undone.
Wes came to and said,
"Please call 911."

Albert made gifts, too. One day, sitting in a rocking chair in my front room, he looked out a south window and said, "Gawddam, John, you're growing a hardwood forest out there. God put grass here, not them gawddam trees."

Albert Wiggins, twenty years into a lifetime of riding horses and looking after cattle.

Albert Wiggins lived his early years in a dugout such as this. Primitive, sure. But like the people who lived here, it got the job done.

When he drove away, I sat in the chair and—across about three hundred acres—I counted nine spindly trees. Two days later, he was back, with a rock he had found, "B-R-O-W-N" carved above a two-inch hole made by a millennium of drips; a horseshoe he had painted green hung through the hole for attachment to an outdoor wall. "Gawddam, John, I'm sorry I said you were growing a hardwood forest out there."

In turn, I advertised his made-up saw shop. Albert had injured his hand somehow, using a chainsaw to notch braces into corner posts, a minor cut but bloody as hell, and I used the sad event as a reason for Albert to start a business. I put posters up at the feed store and at the filling station, each covered in glops of red Magic Marker, the sale prices on his specials of the week—ripping and milling but also bobbing and leeching, bloodletting of any sort—Albert's saw-shop bargains barely legible under the drips of inky hemoglobin.

Albert Wiggins gave up the ghost after eighty-some years of Camel cigarettes and hard rides on cattle drives begun in the fading light of a cornbread moon. I wish only to have seen just some of what he saw—his first bottle of strawberry pop, his first calf weighing six hundred pounds at weaning. Maybe even his old roping buddy lying dead, struck by lightning not a thousand yards from where Albert sharpened posts. Steers running away from him at small-town rodeos, so many of them running free that he quit carrying a pigging string for a while. Would that a man might beg to ride with an old cowboy into pastures that his family had leased for half a century and more. Would that I might know the full-bore strength of the Wiggins seed stock, Albert's dad trying to homestead a ranch, sleeping for a winter in a lean-to under his grandfather's Civil War army blanket.

Because on umpteen hundred mornings, heading out across these hills to work among the grass and the animals in his care, speaking in the tongues of the cowboy, Albert Wiggins, I know now, saw the rough face of God.

Calvin Bewley

He walked down along the creek, dragging a steel rake, its tines thinned and blackened from years of such use. By tradition, or maybe by default, Calvin Bewley began the burn season each year around here. He damned sure did enjoy watching his pasture crinkle into little flames, the reds and yellows dancing, a blackish line of fire among the emerging green of these hills. In the late winter of every spring, Calvin disappeared into the turns, the weeded twists of Bachelor Creek, and it was just as natural and expected to catch a small sight of him there as it was to wink at a whitetail vaulting into the underbrush, to see a tom in full momentary fan.

Calvin's widow, Peg, knew him first at Saturday night dances at Memorial Hall in Eureka—tail gunner Bewley home on furlough, sunburned and handsome, a hero of sorts, straight in a young cowboy's jeans. "He intermissioned better than he danced," she says now, back from bridge club, thoughtful and laughing still, her man buried one mile due west of his horse.

We planned it that way, Mike Wiggins and I. From the kitchen window, Calvin could see where the big black gelding lay, the burial mound still visible after three winters, none as bad as the arctic hell in which Bally fought, from the ground up, the old age that a veterinarian new to town refused to end, what with Calvin on remote vacation, unreachable to give his consent. Mike had brought his rifle that morning we found Bally dead, gone now the gasps and snorts of a good guy's frozen last hours.

Calvin knew such times: the midnight flights in the tunnel hatch of a Catalina PBY5-A, the barrel hot on a .30-caliber machine gun, the twin 1,200-horsepower Pratt & Whitney Wasps slogging a ton of explosives and a bunch of empty beer bottles, terror bombs these, with razor blades inserted in their necks to whistle Japanese soldiers wide awake and afraid. Few of the neighbors and almost none of the townspeople knew of quiet Calvin Bewley's war record until that day up on the hill where we laid him.

We knew him as perhaps the best caretaker of grass and cattle in these parts, a worrier, stewing over every last little detail of moving a set of heifers out of his knee-deep fescue to pots idling their diesels down the road. We knew him as the man Peg first imagined.

An old kid ready, all right, to set the night on fire.

Peggy lives alone now, although her son, Clint, hovers hereabouts, watching over his mother. As does her daughter, Jo, in her way in faraway Connecticut, the passing weathers of the heart holding the three of them close in memory of an old gentleman who waits for them just past an orange hole in the sky.

Hazel and John Wynn

These bluestem hills deal in degrees. They begin at "pretty" and walk off toward "mightily impressive" and "breathtaking" before hauling on through whatever thesaurus you've brought along for the ride. The Wynns, winsome Hazel at age eighty and her five-years-senior brother, John, live somewhere just past "spectacular."

A long time ago, while they lived with relatives in town during the school year, their family's mail was addressed fifteen miles away to Flint Ridge, Kansas, whose makeshift post office stood over on the Lampe Ranch. Rand McNally has never heard of Flint Ridge, Kansas.

Ms. Hazel and Mr. John Wynn are still here, though—not much changed, not much changed at all. Doing well, thanks, on the border of Greenwood and Butler Counties, in Salem Township, on a small ranch surrounded on all sides by the umpteen-acre spreads of big-city landowners who find in the Wynns something like the way it once was and still ought to be around here.

Brother and sister live with electricity but with no inside running water and no telephone down a looping, partially washed-out driveway so far off a far pasture road that the township maintenance people routinely forget they are there. "But we still have to pay the taxes," John says at the threshold of hearing. Soft-spoken but quick to remember and to smile out loud, he lacks his sister's directness. She knows his thinking before it's uttered, and she talks over the top of him.

"I don't have a worry in this world," says Hazel Wynn. "I don't own much more than the old things in this old house, but I don't have a worry. That's because I never borrowed a dollar in my life. If Johnny and I couldn't pay for it, we did without."

Not everyone thinks this way or says such things, she knows.

"A man came through here selling *Capper's Weekly* years ago, and right there on the cover it said 'How To Make It in Farming and Ranching: Get Big.' I bought the magazine so he could win his trip to Hawaii, but I told him he didn't know a thing about agriculture."

With their simple economy, the Wynns have made a living and a two-in-a-million life in this old modern world not far from the homesteaded acreage their grandfather, the Englishman William Wynn, settled in 1869. He favored Galloway cows until their father, John, took the family into the six-month care of framy steers up from Texas, who'd leave Kansas weighing well, well more than half a ton. John Sr. farmed some, too, in the bottoms, and the horses young Johnny knew were far more likely to be harnessed in a

The railroad brought cattle up from Texas to be grazed and then, the steers fat and happy, took them off to market.

team than saddled for a moonlight ride toward the railhead at Rosalia. Out of school early, he worked for twenty years tending the cattle belonging to the McGinnis Ranch a few miles east.

The winsome little anchorwoman again: "But Johnny was no horseman. He has a way with cattle, everyone knows that, but he always looked for the gentlest, slowest old horse. Me? I don't like horses at all. Never did. Don't have any use for them."

In time, John Wynn came home to start his own herd, Hereford cows crossed most years with a black bull. And he and his sister settled into what happens to a family with enough time falling through the cracks. Their parents died at home, cared for and loved till the end by William Wynn's grandchildren. And the cattle too, they knew such care: in the bitter stretches, the mother cows were brought down into the timber around the house, off the exposed hills all around. "He'd leave the house in the middle of the night, in a blizzard, on foot, to go check on them. Two and three times a night he would go to make sure they were safe," says the sister who could make no coffee strong enough to settle her nerves nor hot enough to warm him before daybreak, when he had walked the darkness down.

As recently as 1979, the blizzards came, and the roads were blocked beyond motor graders, and for three weeks, sister and brother lived beyond human contact until the D9 Cats came. "We never wanted for anything," John remembers, the cooling cave full of potatoes and home-canned fruits and their own good beef. "One of our cows calved right at the beginning of the storm, and the calf was pretty well iced-up by the time we found her and got her into the house. We didn't lose a one though. Not a one."

A foreign world is coming directly at sister and brother, dirtying up their doorstep. It comes head-on, homeward in the form of *sericea Lespideza*, the insidious, government-induced legume now threatening to consume these hills and their grass. Ranchers around here fight it with strong chemicals, goats densely pastured and research centered on a particular webworm.

John Wynn had never seen *sericea Lespideza* until a neighbor drove him over a few miles to identify its advance. His sister, sweet and strong as a Vidalia onion, has already begun her fight. On their walks across an ancestral ranch, Ms. Hazel Wynn stoops now and then. She stoops and, with her garden shears, takes a stand against this newest danger to the only place she and Johnny have ever known.

GERALD ROBERTS

Just south of Talmage, Kansas, a three-time all-around champion of the rodeo world is driving home in a pickup the color of cowboy hurt. He does not blink. If he happens to wave, the oncoming motorist must be very, very alert to the greeting. Outside an arena, Gerald Roberts is not given to large, showy gestures. Gerald Roberts drives home this evening wearing a belt buckle that no other cowboy on this earth has earned the right to wear. He travels in a purplish, late-model pickup with a chrome roll bar mounted in the bed, two, maybe three, hundred pounds of protection that stands like the firmament over his hatted head. The people who have seen Gerald Roberts ride would find the roll bar an anomaly, a little inside joke on an eighty-year-old cowboy who first rode professionally at the age of thirteen. The roll bar hovers in a way that no helmet, no flak jacket ever protected him in the way-gone days when he climbed onto carnival bulls and broncs for a hayfield Wild West show every thirty minutes. All day long. For ten bucks a week. And free food.

Here's who's at home.

Pat, first and last and always, wife and business partner in charge of spoiling cattle and wildfowl and, as his turn comes round, Gerald Roberts.

And ghosts, the house is full of ghosts. The subjects of ten thousand stories. Cowboy names that roll like summer thunder: Tibbs; Shoulders; Linderman; Gerald's own older brother, the late world champion Ken Roberts. Gerald rode with these boys. Sat evenings with them, fifteen or so broken ribs among them just about average in those one-night cheap hotels. Felt, too, their simple school-kid joy at eight seconds of life interrupted, detached, alone and unafraid in the face of contrived, but no less real, mayhem, no less genuine fury.

Home now sitting in his easy chair, his eyes misted up with tiredness and remembering, he says again how he hoed bindweed with his dad for a dollar a day…how he took thirteen dollars of his pay and, with his pop's permission and wearing a rodeo shirt handmade by his mother, hitchhiked to Perry, Iowa, for a bull ride in Clyde Miller's Wild West Extravaganza… how he lived a little bit of heaven there for a time until he got caught up in his rigging and the bull knocked him unconscious, and he spent eight hours in a coma, enough time for his employer to discover that his top hand was but thirteen years old, and Mr. Miller shipped him right back home, the thirteen dollars still in his pocket…how he and Ken hoboed into Nevada to ride feral horses and found themselves running from railroad detectives instead…how it took him five miles to wheel down a dozen boxcars on a seventy-mile-per-hour train to a speed at which even he would jump off back home in Strong City, Kansas…how he became the very first pro rodeo cowboy to model and endorse Wrangler jeans—brother Ken meantime appearing in full-page, illustrated ads for Camel cigarettes titled "Four-Legged Fury," a four-color Ken saying, "Camels suit my T-bone [taste-bone] to a T,"…how he won the North American Championship in Calgary in 1950…how he and Casey Tibbs most likely invented flying in between matinees a thousand miles apart, a twin-engine Cessna helping them make four rodeos a week until lightning struck a hangar in Colorado Springs and burned up Gerald's plane and twelve more besides, an act of God saving Gerald's life from a mechanical contraption that threatened him in a way an enraged farm animal never could…how he became a Hollywood stunt man, doubling for Arthur Kennedy in *Lusty Men*; for Glenn Ford, who became his close friend; for Jack Lemmon in *Cowboy*, a movie in which he played both Lemmon's stunt double and the Comanche who shoots and kills him… how he worked in *Gunsmoke*, *Maverick*, *Have Gun—Will Travel* and *Rin Tin Tin*…how throughout his stunt and acting career, he uttered just one word on screen, in the TV mystery *Boston Blackie*, playing a farm kid with two bloodhounds hired to track down a bad guy, and Gerald rears himself up and says into the camera, "Him?"...how in 1965, the Cowboy Hall of Fame asked him on in.

In a home of his and Pat's own devising, sitting next to a spring-fed pond that has never once gone dry, he's entitled to pull a boot from a foot belonging, in a way, to him. The color of the pickup parked right outside, swollen and misshapen in the manner of an NFL injury not thirty minutes old, Gerald's ankle hangs in the middle distance. A trophy wreck for sure.

The bronc stepped just so that night in the largest city in the world, and a shard of bone pinned a Flint Hills cowboy to the mud floor of Madison Square Garden. Through the skin, of course, as all compound fractures must do to earn their buckle, and through a pretty good boot. All the way into the used dirt of an eastern rodeo, that bone stuck like a spike, and the first doctor to look at the bits of skin holding it on to the rest of Gerald went right away to the A-word.

Michael Diane, MD, just back from field surgery in World War II, entertained other ideas, told some dry-mouthed cowboys to carry Gerald to Poly Clinic Hospital just across the street, gave him a spinal tap and commenced to wash the floppy thing like a dirty sock. One, per Gerald, "miraculous surgery" and right at one hundred shots of penicillin later, Dr. Diane walked up to the world champion and said, "Mr. Roberts, I think we're going to save your leg." On October 25, 1946, Dr. Diane told Gerald that he might walk but that he would never ride again. On February 25, 1947, Gerald Roberts stepped on a saddle bronc in Tucson.

After a long time, the bravery and the bravado settled into the day-to-day, and Gerald went back to marketing. In the years before 2005, when he rode off on that granddaddy highball freight, he made and sold chaps, chinks, saddlebags, saddle covers and feed and cantle bags—working stuff plain and fancy for Saturday night and Monday morning alike. Because, away from home, a cowboy needs some protection.

Some roll bars and, as the need comes round, some penicillin.

NEWT THORNTON

His mother, two sisters, four brothers and he tried to get on the Dawes Roll, which would declare them official members of the Chickasaw Nation, deserving of their share of the money and land the last treaty had made certain. With not much luck, not much luck at all. His mother, Isabel Fowler, had married James Andrew Thornton a bit too late, and there came a son, born a thorn unto his flesh. Illegitimate for sure but the favorite in spite of, or maybe because of, his illegitimacy, over the next some years, this newcomer, half-brother little Andy, could do no wrong as Newt, the oldest, felt random, awful maternal fury. His brother Chester remembers Newt as profane and loud in the face of the latest injustice, and one day he just slapped that Andy flat silly. Whereupon, Isabel turned to her husband and asked him, please, to kill her firstborn. Young Newt Thornton could recite from memory, often did declaim "The Rime of the Ancient Mariner," Coleridge's longish poem addressing, among other matters of life and death, abrupt decision-making. He took off.

He followed a cattle drive coming through Springer, Oklahoma, the steers trailing their way north, Newt a hand at fourteen but too young for the Great War beginning that year (1917), and he went just as far as he could with that little horse. They made it to Shidler, with winter coming quick, and he found a job, firing a wood oven at a bakery, that carried him through. Ranch work then with the banker Eugene Shidler, who gave his name to the boomtown that grew up at the Burbank Field, one of the largest oil finds in the nation at the time. Maybe Newt Thornton knew a guy name of Clark Gable, who worked as a roustabout in the fields, with ten thousand other hard-livers ensconced in the tents, huts and makeshift houses of early Shidler, Oklahoma.

He hired on at the Corbin Ranch outside Stonewall and stayed there four years or so. Then, for more than thirty years, he worked for the Drummonds, his pay $125 per month to manage the ranch—top wages when he started, $125 a month not so much when he retired. But the Drummonds gave him access to the Pioneer Store, their mercantile in Hominy, with groceries, hardware, furniture and dry goods. "My mother would really have liked to buy a dress somewhere else," his daughter says. The Drummond family, aristocratic and kind, with educations that began up in Stillwater in boarding schools, way before enrollment age at Oklahoma A&M, knew the fierce, my-way scope of his cowboying, and they gave him the pasture for his own growing herd. Newt and Maudie, the one woman stout enough to stand up to his runaway gruff, the great soft heart of the grass itself just beneath, lived on that ranch and raised their little girl, and Jackie—she stole him clean away. She went with him everywhere, a shadow among the cowhands, and once, when her daddy had some extended business away from the ranch, so outraged at his

Newt Thornton (standing), Osage cowboy of the old school, working calves on the Drummond Ranch.

absence that she ripped into Flossie Flirt, her doll no longer to be bundled up and taken with her on her father's way to do the chores.

In 1962, he took off again, up into the Flint Hills of Kansas, nine miles north of Eureka, where he brought his cows and Angus bulls as fine as any left behind on the Drummond place. He paid cash for one-thousand-some acres of primo bluestem with Bachelor Creek running through, large ponds, good fence—the ranch where I married his granddaughter.

In time, Maudie passed and, caught by his family chipping ice for those cows in a December blizzard, he was forced to move to town, but not before he had cowboyed for another fifteen years. He took a lady friend, and he shared his snorted wisdom with her as that dear woman nodded in barely spoken assent. He sat straight-backed till the end, an Osage horseman of the old ways.

I remember the last two sentences he spoke to me. Lying in a semiprivate room in the rural hospital, with a man whose pain had led to all-night moans and the roommate moved somewhere else, Newt told me, "I like to do my suffering in silence." And then on the way out the door, Annie kissing her granddad for what she knew to be the final time, he called out, "Best go and make yourself some memories."

That old cowboy—he ran away from home for a reason.

PAUL SR. AND LAURA HYNER SEELEY

Make no mistake, the schoolteacher Laura Hyner taught for the test there at the Friend's School (founded by Cecil Friend) in rural Lookout, Oklahoma, in the 1927–28 educational year. Falling in love with a cowboy who was kicked out of seventh grade a dozen years before, Monday through Friday, she walked to the one-room school two miles north from the little house Mr. Cecil provided for his children's teacher. And she taught to the test, all right.

Some sample questions:

> *Arithmetic: District No. 33 has a valuation of $35,000. What is the necessary levy to carry on a school seven months at $50 per month, and have $104 for incidentals?*
> *U.S. History: Relate the causes and results of the Revolutionary War.*
> *Orthography: What are the following, and give examples of each: trigraph, subvocals, diphthong, cognate letters, linguals?*
> *Geography: How do you account for the extremes of climate in Oklahoma?*

The requirements for graduating from eighth grade in those days were roughly commensurate with the difficulties of rural life in general back then. Hard times, hard people. The gentle Laura understood her

Laura Hyner lived in this little house, from which she walked two miles north to teach country school.

prospects, asked for nothing more from the cowman from down the road who had bought the box supper she had so specially prepared for the social the Sunday night before.

She could see the life before her, a ranch wife now, the teaching job gone by law upon her marriage. She understood the working cowboy's lot, most especially in these dust-blown days, the horseback wages of a hand with aspirations toward a herd of his own. And so, Paul Seeley's auctioneer's certificate earned, Laura clerked at his little sales facility across the state line in Coldwater, Kansas. She watched the redistribution of the well-used shop tools, of the occasional cow-calf pair, of finally the wedding china of one poor family to another. A cattle deal gone way south, they thought of themselves as poor, too. And so, nothing to be done but work another hard day without, not once, looking up.

She followed him in time back to Kansas's largest city, holding on to the ranch at Lookout, while he worked at the commission barn in Wichita, earning money enough to support the dream out west. Their little boy grown to be a cowboy himself, she followed along in the car as they drove those one-hundred-some steers just up out of Chihuahua the eighty miles from Medicine Lodge all the way to the railroad siding at Edith at the edge of the Okie salt flats. She slept with her husband and her son at friends' houses along the trail, the cattle penned for the night right outside. She sat alone on the side of the frozen road, as her Pauls—Junior and Senior—roped a steer, drug it across iced-up Highway 160, the horses somehow staying afoot, the other steers inching along behind the reluctant, twice-lassoed lead. Soon enough, she had seen it all.

All but Australia.

Their retirement come, the herd of cows on its eventual route to ownership by their only granddaughter, Paul began to mow lawns. He bought a tommy lift for his red S-10 Chevy pickup to maneuver the zero–turning radius hot rod from jobsite to Woodward, Oklahoma jobsite, widows waiting mostly, octogenarians taken with the courtly behavior, the meticulous work habits of the old cowboy who cut their grass at a price they simply could not refuse. Paul Seeley Sr. earned just over $7,500 his first summer on the job. In October, he and Laura headed off down under, at the ages of eighty and seventy-eight respectively. About time, they figured, to see the cattle business from the other side of the world.

In cleaning her mother-in-law's last home before Laura went off to the assisted-living facility, Jackie Seeley found a handwritten note inside an embroidered handkerchief. The note, from a cowboy in love in 1928, read in part, "I don't have much now, but I promise that someday I'll be worth something."

Unwieldy proposition, worth.

In her tested schoolteacher's heart, long before the cows came home for good, Laura Hyner Seeley, she knew something about value. In the dearest, deep-down freshness of those long-gone words, maybe she knew exactly what, someday, it all might mean.

An Eternal Spring

On the treeless prairie, fire can come nine miles from nowhere, a roaring, dry grass–fueled dragon of ferocious heat and indefensible fury. Wildfire can threaten rural families today with a windborne vengeance scarcely less brutal than that which their great-grandparents faced. But a wildfire—the product of lightning or careless welding or, sadly, thrillseekers throwing matches—stands very, very different from "the burn." The burn is a land-management tool with natural consequences that lead to more productive pastures and heavier yearlings.

The burn remains one of the principal tools of Flint Hills ranchers—the original conservationists and everyday environmentalists.

Where wildfire is erratic and destructive, the burn is planned, controlled and timed to take advantage of native grasses' ability to withstand the fire and weeds' susceptibility to it. The details of the burn accumulate in a military sort of preparedness, in an assessment of weather in general and winds in particular, in truck-mounted water tanks and huge sprayers pulled behind tractors, in the troops equipped with rakes and paddles for beating out little fingers of flame, in the carefully planned backfires and the sequestering of livestock, in the county regulations and the state laws that control the fires' setting. Without these preparations, fire, potentially the cattleman's and his animals' best friend, can become in an instant an implacable enemy.

The early-April burn begins with fire sticks, ten-foot strands of galvanized pipe with bent and welded handles and, at the other end, partially plugged plumbing elbows, the pipe full of gasoline trickling out of a drilled crack in the plug. "Stringing fire," the cowboys call it, homemade napalm bouncing along behind the walking stringers, stringers on four-wheelers, stringers on the hard backs of feed trucks, all sending stripes of head fire upwind so that heat and convection are dispersed, and no single line is allowed to cross the break.

When properly applied, fire benefits the grassland and the animals that graze it. The burn has always been about protein—and profitability.

Kansas State University's School of Range Management demonstrated that yearling steers grazed on pastures burned in late April or early May gained twenty-six pounds more than steers grazed on unburned pastures. The study showed further that the upper five feet of soil in the burned pasture retained two to three more inches of moisture than in the unburned. The burn also controls weeds and undesirable perennial forbs, broadleaf plants with varied palatability and nutritional value for cattle.

When the weather cooperates with sufficient rain before the burn and warm sunny days immediately afterward, the yearlings can move onto the burned pastures within a week, sometimes sooner. Their noses black for a few days, they are most certainly smiling, the nutrients in the new grass spiking upward toward Memorial Day.

In cattle country, before the green comes the black; before the harvest of the precious grasslands comes fire.

Spreading like spring.

I've always believed that gratitude makes us human, and these hills ask that we look down every bit as much as we look out and up. A pasture is best judged from a vertical aspect; the horizontal can confuse and wrongly enhance. So I stand now just north of the house, where if I wait long enough, a blind creature will stare up at me, thankfully, from his home.

The armadillo is an anomaly of creation. Essentially toothless, covered with bony calcium plates, its scientific name is a paradoxical combination of two nouns and an adjective meaning "Mexican turtle rabbit." Always born as an identical quadruplet, the armadillo lives on insects, worms and vegetable matter. They say the meat tastes like pork. Death-bound, the 'dillo is a carrier: one in three cases of leprosy transmitted each year in the United States comes as a direct result of touching an armadillo. Of the twenty varieties of the animal in God's creation, only one lives here in cowboy country—the nine-banded version, all striped up with, until just recently, no place to go. Our lucky guy is flourishing, especially now that the species has figured out a means of crossing Highway 99 in far southern Kansas. Even though they can jump five feet straight up and run a full fifteen miles an hour, migrant turtle-rabbits do not deal well with the American automobile. For years, their calcified carcasses littered a particularly murderous stretch of 99, running from Arkansas City clear over to Joplin.

Their improved travel skills have now brought the creatures to Greenwood County to confront life out here on the occasionally snow-covered plain. Armadillos hate the cold, so I found no surprise in his burrow beneath, irony of ironies, my firewood stack. The winter didn't kill him. I found a week ago his scratchings in a dried-out lawn, and this evening I wait to see him face to face, him all voodoo and surreal, up from his travels in the gothic south.

Again tonight, I live in the nimbus of protecting angels, next door to a weird little creature bent to his bugged night's work. Out here, people make plans. A lot of life happens in the meantime. We work hard, and then we rodeo.

When the dust settles, ranch rodeos amount most of all to contests of efficiency, that most valued cowboy virtue—how to do good work quickly and well. Two buckaroos vaccinating heifers accelerate the girls through the chute, because they understand that the stress of confinement often exceeds the stress of the puncture wound. Stress diminishes animal performance. The rewards of the hands' efficiency come in dollars pocketed on shipping day. No such rewards, economic or otherwise, wait for the nameless employees of the state laboring in, say, the Department of Motor Vehicles.

The bureaucracy rules from an overstuffed recliner at full, flat inertia. At its best, the bureaucracy ensures mediocrity. At its worst, it ensures the regulated distribution of misery. Wrapped in red tape, bundled for maximized effect, the long-term effects of rule by officials slog toward inefficiency, waste and corruption. L'Enfant's plan for our nation's set-aside capital, its only district, decreed that no building should stand taller than the Capitol, and so the bureaucracy sprawls, its cubicles stretching for miles in columned four-story stone structures that overpower but do not inspire. And the governmental buildings, the ridiculous acreage absorptive in August's hundred-degree heat, pretty much just sit there. As do their occupants. Faceless, pointless, useless, neither here nor there in an annual expenditure of a trillion dollars extracted from folks who pound fence posts for a living.

Grady Gibb, all-around cowboy, up in a ranch rodeo, demonstrating that ranching is a team sport.

The most efficient of hunters, this hawk waits for the spring fires to force his prey into a narrow waterway.

The bureaucracy demands the concentration of unproven, unprovable certainty amid the diffusion of responsibility. And volume. Big government demands lots of volume as measured both in decibels and in word count, an endless proliferation of legislated gibberish, the simple and the sequential complicated beyond recognition. Arrogance and illogic slopped into the Congressional Record. Questions about the definition of "is," the easiest of all intransitive verbs. Campaign promises requiring more time to utter than to break. The truth gasping under the leaden weight of senatorial posturing. Everyone in Washington, D.C., talking at once, blind men sneering over the cardboard rules they've made.

My father-in-law is a rancher, the boss of the spread on which my cows raised their fat black babies. A fourth-generation cowboy, his degree in animal husbandry from Oklahoma A&M earned from ROTC and a wrestling scholarship, he ranches pretty much his every waking hour. He does not hunt. Or fish. Or play golf. His September vacation invariably involves a drive through some distant cow country—Florida last year, its traditions of the cowman identical to and so different from the tallgrass Okie ways of his thirty thousand days. Vacation days and workdays alike, he studies. Eighty years into a singly focused career, and he's still learning, going to every class on multiple-species grazing, every seminar on veterinary pharmaceuticals, every grass tour in a ten-county area. He subscribes to a dozen agricultural publications, and he reads them daily. Mostly he rides this ranch, and he looks around. Maybe a cross-fence here. A new concrete waterer there.

Unlike the politicians who would misguide him or the bureaucrats who would rule him, Paul Seeley admits his mistakes, corrects them without anyone's notice, and sets about every new day with wide, vigorous eyes. My father-in-law goes to school at almost ninety years of age because a new wrinkle on an old truth might give him the wherewithal for a new pickup on down the road. Government employees who already know it all, members of a union every unelected one, labor unbeknownst to anyone but themselves and supervisors who cannot fire them from jobs that won't ever serve a purpose beyond a paycheck extorted from good men on horseback.

For too many people, work has lost its purpose because its end is not in sight. The bureaucracy will create busyness for itself, something no real cowboy would ever, ever do. And waste, that sad story—it repeats itself.

With armadillos in residence on her perfect place, too, my friend Melba knew no use for the District of Columbia.

PART II

LOOKING DOWN: THE WORK AT HAND

Melba Fechter

She works this morning, as she has for the past forty-seven years, in the shop beside the sign "Melba's Upholstery." At eighty-one, she has survived lung cancer and the loss of the man she loved for sixty years, old Roy, the carpenter, the ranch hand, the farmer, the maintainer. The little house and the sheds surrounding Melba's Upholstery rest in an all-around immaculateness that only daily spit and routine polish can achieve. The paint on these buildings gleams blue-white, the flowers bloom and the grass stands short again today. Melba Fechter believes in "doing things right." She works hard and long as a natural matter of fact, she does.

Her father spoke often his profane opinion that "if a man doesn't have sweat running down the crack of his ass, he ain't worth a damn." On his farm, a wood stove heated the house. Melba milked cows by the light of a kerosene lamp. She drove a tractor, pulled a plow. She threatened to leave home when she was but twelve, her will and her oomph obvious even then. Working with her dad in the wheat field, she had allowed, as she remembers, "maybe a cupful" of grain to fall to the ground from the box wagon she was attending, as he augured a load from the tractor-pulled combine. He yelled, "I'm raising a gawddamned piss-brained kid," and off she went. Her dad changed his attitude over the dinner hour, and by that afternoon, he approved the work habits of his little daughter and persuaded her to unpack her impromptu bag.

She finally left the farm outside of Quincy, Kansas, to enroll in business college in Wichita, where she moved into the YWCA. A blind date arranged by her friend Lorna introduced her to Roy Fechter, who on their first date took her to the Calico Cat, the biggest nightclub in town. When six months later Lorna married her man, Bud, with Melba and Roy as witnesses, at the moment of pronouncement of man-and-wife, young Roy fainted dead away. He awoke and, a few minutes later, gave Melba a diamond ring.

They married on December 4, 1948, Melba's nineteenth birthday. Roy built a bathroom onto the little house they bought just off Highway 99, south of Hamilton. He continued his carpentering, bought some Angus cattle, hauled some sheep over from his folks' place, owned "those old milk cows, Guernseys," and for a while, the Fechters had a milking machine. Melba pulled calves, delivered lambs.

One evening, Herb Rockhill, for whom Roy worked weekends at the cattle sale in Eureka, stopped by to see the Fechters and found Melba in the barn, milking a dozen cows by hand. "You hold a cow's tail down when you're milking, or she'll raise it and do her business," Melba teaches. "Well, I was talking to Herb, and I didn't have the tail held tight, and she plopped and then wrapped that tail around my neck. Why did Herb have to be here to see that, I want to know!"

Roy beat cancer of the larynx, brought on at least in part, in his wife's considered opinion, by the thirty hours straight he'd work at the sale barn, whooping and hollering, moving a thousand head into the pens, then in and out of the ring, a few steers at a time, canner cows bunched to sell fast, Roy hoarse beyond speaking by the time he made it home to Melba and Danny and little Cindy. Before the work ended, Roy's own barn burned down, and the sheep shed blew away in the sheer winds, which come fifty miles an hour around here. With two kids and the times hard, Melba looked for something to do beyond the slopping of hogs.

The upholstery business began with Melba "doing a chair" for herself, and then visiting down on the Sutton Ranch, a friend pointed to a piece in need of repair, and Danny, aged five, said, "My momma can do it." On their first business call, delivering the professional tools of the trade, the guys from Oklahoma Supply said to Melba, "If you get started, the customers won't let you quit." "Quit," a foreign and stupid word right there, beside the point of what she needed to do.

Now her work sits in an elegant living room in California and on the lanai of a Hawaiian mansion. Melba recovered "a big old chair and ottoman" in the precise colorings of the Green Bay Packers. Beyond those pieces and the white dining chairs in the next room over, now two years paid for, encased in plastic and waiting on the owner's retrieval...beyond them...Melba Fechter can't think of any special jobs, any projects that stand out and apart from five decades of coming essentially every day out here to tuck and to pull and to tuft, to sew and to hammer, to align once more a seam with a sworn craftswoman's laser eye.

When her own cancer came, "I got over it, so I could look after Roy," Melba says, this job intended straight for her from some kingdom to come. "He'd go nuts if I wasn't around here." This comes from a woman who understands her place in the universe. But Roy was undone by carcinomas that "bloomed up all of a sudden," massive in his lungs at Thanksgiving time, quick to his liver and his brain, dead on Father's Day. "When I saw that Roy was going to die, I started to prepare myself. This gal up the road, her husband passed away, she says all she can do is cry. She cries and cries and cries, and I said to her 'Glenda, what in hell good does it do?'" Even though, now and then, Melba herself needs some outside help. With a behemoth of a ranch-oak sleeper sofa in the shop, she required first the UPS man and then Karla, "a good old girl, the meter reader for Westar, from up by Virgil," to muscle the sofa into position for its refurbishment.

Now, in her ninth decade of cutting grass and over the imagined objections of her late husband, she has purchased a riding mower. Her daughter-in-law said as much there in front of the sales clerk at Bluestem Farm and Ranch Supply in Emporia. "Roy wouldn't like this," said the daughter-in-law, remembering his preference for the quality of cut that only a twenty-two-inch push mower can deliver. But Melba said, "It's my money!" and the rider came home, followed in quick succession by a pull-behind cart ("So I can haul limbs to my woodpile") and a tool that she calls a "grabber"—one of those long sticks with a claw at the far end ("So I can pick up my yard without getting off my mower").

But hold on a minute here. Just a damned minute. Almost out of sight, back by the garage, something unseemly. Not immaculate, this set of rusted bedsprings. I think I know what the springs mean, but confirmation is called for. And so I'm back out of the truck with one last question for my pal: "Melba, are you tying on to those bedsprings to drag the rock in your driveway?"

And from deep in her shop, her tiny shoulders squared inside a white sweatshirt with a sunflower on its front, her fingers going haywire with

This north-leaning tree stands emblematic of both prevailing southerly breezes and strong people at home in a hard, hard wind.

A foundation is restoring Pioneer Bluffs as a center for experiential education about both the history and the future of the Flint Hills.

arthritis, her head bent again to the task at hand, and there in the small of her back, a bead of sweat beginning to form, Melba Fechter says, "Yep. The old lady has to save herself any way she can. Any way she can."

THE UMBEHRS

He met Eileen in high school in Singapore. Keen enrolled at the American School because of his father's job with Dresser Magcobar, the oil business taking the family all over the world. Eileen attended there as well, her dad a vice-president of 3M. Keen followed her back to Minnesota and won her hand, and the new Mr. and Mrs. Umbehr quickly moved back to Kansas, away from the snarl and the noise of Minneapolis to quiet, lovely, simple Alma, where his father had been born, where he had spent summers on the farm since seventh grade.

Keen took a job with the Wabaunsee County Weed Department, supporting his growing family as best he could in a town where human needs are inexpensively met, basic human wants even more so. Two years into the spraying of ditches, Keen persuaded Eileen that hauling trash was the sure-fire monetary way to go. They wheedled a loan for fifty-large, bought a used compactor, and Keen went to work removing refuse from Alma, Alta Vista, Eskridge, Harveyville, Maple Hill, McFarland and Paxico—all seven of the county's towns on a contract with the commissioners. He worked ten years on that truck, never once missing a day, not once late on a pickup, working through sickness and injury and mechanical breakdowns and not a single customer complaint in a decade's worth of trucking the ruined and the rotting.

On April 13, 1989, a column called "My Perspective" appeared for the first time in the *Alma Signal-Enterprise*, Keen Umbehr, columnist. The first local issue to be discussed involved the closing of the Wabaunsee County landfill. Over the next two years, "My Perspective" challenged the Wabaunsee County Commission's business practices, the secrecy of some of its dealings and the peculiar intermixture of personal, familial and governmental relationships perhaps inevitable in a county of just 6,922 residents. Keen Umbehr spoke the blunt words of the downright man he has always been, grinning out loud as he tweaked the mildly corrupt, the no-big-deal wrongdoing of the way it has always been done around here.

In 1991, the county commissioners had read enough, and for reasons most assuredly their own, they fired Solid Waste Systems, Keen and Eileen

Umbehr its owners. In 1996, the justices of the United States Supreme Court voted 7-2 that the commissioners had violated Keen's civil rights—a brash trash hauler's voice heard in the highest court in the land. The decision established the legal principle that independent contractors have the same First Amendment rights and protections as government employees. The Freedom Forum awarded Keen its Free Spirit Award for 1998, giving national recognition to a Kansas guy who refused to be shoved around.

He sold his trash company and went back to college at the age of forty, rooming with his son, Josh, then a freshman at Kansas State. In 2005, Keen graduated from Washburn University School of Law.

For a time, he served as the public defender in Junction City, Kansas, next door to Fort Riley, home of the First Division and its young soldiers ready to fling some jack around in pursuit of a good time off post. Keen Umbehr once appeared before a judge who had seen this stagecraft before, as the barrister Umbehr pled "attempted speeding" for a GI client going much, much too fast.

His case a landmark of free speech in America, here was a neighbor's take on Keen's future: "It may well be that Keen Umbehr will never be a very good lawyer—too moral, too righteous, too concerned with right and wrong. I warned him fifteen years ago that the practice of law in the United States had nothing to do with justice and everything to do with process."

The neighbor was quickly proved right. Keen faced ethics charges for once again seeking hard truth. Seems he took a reporter with him into the Topeka Correctional Facility, identifying the man simply as his "assistant." The reporter then wrote a series of truth-tellings about routine, forcible servicing of male guards by female inmates, about inmates and staff being forced to remove asbestos from the facility with no training, no masks, no good air to breathe. The Kansas Department of Corrections filed sudden complaints of ethics violations, seeking to have the young lawyer disbarred. Justice done again, those charges were dismissed, and Keen has now taken his longtime fight for transparency and accountability from our government to a new venue.

The man is running for governor of Kansas on the ticket of the Libertarian Party. His son, Josh, now the founder of a nationally prominent concierge family medicine practice, stands beside his dad as candidate for lieutenant governor. The Umbehrs' platform could not be more populist, more in tune with the rugged individualism of Alma in the Flint Hills of Kansas: defense of constitutionally guaranteed freedoms, the exercise of fiscal responsibility in the reduction of government's oppressive size, protection of personal property rights, focused preservation of the Second Amendment, passage of the Fair Tax and, in Keen's words, "unleashing your family's potential by implementing a zero income tax rate for all Kansans." Keen speaks of "liberty and prosperity for all." In that attempted-speeding mindset of his, he means it.

After the high court's ruling, amid the tumult of a wildman's law practice, in 2008, Eileen Umbehr wrote a book, *Small Town Showdown*, detailing in 485 pages the "true story of a trashman's battle for free speech that led him from a Kansas town to the United States Supreme Court." In public defense, in squabbles with the bureaucracy as in political campaigns, a man just has to feel the sweet presence of a knowing, daily guardian angel.

This quicksilver woman has journaled the days, the ongoing ways of their Singapore high-school crush, and now she turns out across these sacred hills, this eternal grass, and Eileen Umbehr thinks of their lives together. A new, ninth grandson just baptized, Eileen Umbehr writes of justice served. Of how, as our turn comes round, a guiding spirit looks down, sees attempted speeding at every intersection and watches as each of us finds essentially, precisely what we deserve.

THE HUBBARDS

Sharon Hubbard is a horsewoman from way, way back. Her husband, Alan, made himself a cowman. So there appears a sign on their front gate, which reads, "This ranch is dedicated, first and foremost, to the comfort and safety of the animals who live here. If you have a problem with that, maybe you should leave."

With priorities in line, the Hubbards—genuinely friendly people—will serve as ideal examples of careful ranch managers, showing in their multispecies approach to profitability the way that successful operations are proceeding in these most difficult economic times. In these times of increasing federal regulation of agriculture—as if such an increase were possible.

Consider: the most profitable business ever to take place on the Hubbards' Shannon Creek Herefords and Quarter Horses involved mice. Mice. Sharon was raising white mice to be sold for a dollar per rodent to both research facilities as laboratory animals and to zoos and herpetariums as food for snakes. The mice were fat and prolific, content in the care of a woman devoted to their comfort and safety. The Hubbards were making money hand over fistfuls of mice, but—turns out—snakes in captivity in this country may eat only properly licensed food; research is somehow compromised by test animals lacking governmental approval, and the ever-intrusive, too-often-hostile United States Department of Agriculture shut her down.

Back, then, to more traditional ranch animals. At one time, the Hubbards leased more than five thousand acres of native grass—and eight hundred acres of brome and old cropland—onto which they'd bring 1,500 custom stockers from early May to early August. Steep and rough as it is picturesque, the deeded property on their ranch stretches into the breaks along Tuttle Creek Reservoir. Alan and Sharon have been using a management-intensive grazing system that maximizes pounds of beef produced per acre; their intensively grazed, frequently rotated grass produces twice the poundage as their extensively grazed acres.

This grazing system—in which grass can be rotated but watering points cannot—demanded that the Hubbards make a substantial investment in bringing water to the paddocks. They dug a new well. On a high hill, they erected a storage tank holding ten thousand gallons of fresh, clean water. They laid well more than a mile of gravity-fed waterline to three watering tanks, easily serving up to seven hundred head of yearlings. Then came fencing of the ranch's ponds to prevent erosion from heavy cattle traffic and to maintain water quality for later use.

The ranch's profitability increased significantly. "I made three dollars an acre on conventionally grazed grass compared to twenty-five dollars an acre on the management-intensive rotational grass," Alan says. "What's more, I also achieve a seven dollar per acre winter benefit by being able to graze stockpiled grass with my cow herd." Flexibility, reliability, profitability and environmental responsibility—all the characteristics of carefully managed ranching here.

The Hubbards have also worked hard to eliminate as much machinery as possible; cattle and horses can harvest the forages just fine. Careful rotation of the cattle, coupled with all of their hoof action, controls weeds, and of course, the Hubbards burn their pastures and cut out the red cedars by hand as necessary.

Right there is the brief summary of one family's way of maximizing their stewardship and their careful use of the land. Alan and Sharon Hubbard came to such an understanding across a lifetime of imagination and hard work. They found their ways to each other across the long and convoluted path that small-town romance sometimes takes.

Sharon grew up on a dairy farm, the work there incessant, vacation a distant and silly idea. She met Alan at the Potawatomie County State Fair in 1967, when they were eighth-graders. Her show heifer took the blue ribbon. Young Alan's groomed young cow came in second place. He had spent his childhood on the rural places of his grandma, his aunts and uncles, and he took his lessons there with all the seriousness of a young man on his way.

Sharon too. After high school, she took off. She traveled and traveled some more—no destination too far, no journey too long. She moved about for ten years, and then she came home, and she has stayed, vacations again a distant idea, home the only place to be. She waitressed on her return, and a second-place cowboy ate his share of meals thereabouts. They married after an appropriate number of restaurant visits. Then they moved into Sharon's old family home, her five siblings gone clean away, and nobody but the newlyweds to run the cows and keep up the Nelson place.

Joseph showed up in 1987. He lives now just a few miles from the house where he grew up. He and his wife, Shelby, work alongside his folks. Shelby also brings money back to the ranch from her time as a beautician at Studio Five in Westmoreland. "Behind every successful ranch is a wife who works in town," as the bromide goes.

The Hubbards have built a life with the passing of the days that bring the work. In lunar cycles come the changing tasks of a diversified agricultural endeavor: there lie dozens of irons in the Shannon Creek branding fire. In this family's work, month after month, comes the innovation required for profitability, the steadfastness demanded by a changing marketplace and—always, always—the ethic. The subtle joys of an active life supported by an ethic of purposeful labor.

Joseph spends January in the barn, show goats being born all over these pens. He checks the nannies and their kids every three hours through the night, on into first light when he's already grinding hay for the heifers. Joseph's dad, on his way to work at the dairy barn at K-State, drops in for yet another look at the goats. In between other jobs, Joseph and Alan cut hedge and locust. Most daylight hours in the winter involve the installation of irrigation pivots, a contract with a local dealer that Joseph calls a lifesaver. The job ensures cash flow for two families used to infrequent ranch paydays. Alan's job in Manhattan—eight-hour shifts on Mondays, Tuesdays, Thursdays and Saturdays—means health insurance and a retirement fund, and he is straightforward about his familial reasons for the job. On Fridays, he works for the Manhattan Commission Company as a field hand.

Meantime, Sharon is cooking for a neighbor with multiple sclerosis, delivering pureed, all-organic meals three days a week. She keeps the house, does the chores and carries the quarter-horse business. Most days, Alan is home before four o'clock—first job done, now ready to haul round bales to the horses and the cow herd—"everyone stays out in the country all winter," says Alan. All the Hubbards will be working in the cold until after dark, some days way, way past dark.

February brings but little change: now the ewes have replaced the nannies in the barn, and the same rigorous schedule of checking the new deliveries—two hundred ewes synchronized to lamb at roughly the same time. "We have to deal with the confusion," Joseph says. "With seven or eight lambs just born in a pen with twenty ewes, we have to match up mom and baby in a hurry. But we have them safe and dry and out of the wind." The work in the construction of center-pivot irrigation systems continues.

Hard to imagine, but the Hubbard to-do list shortens a bit in March, with lambs and kids fattening and happy in the wayward weather of late winter in Kansas—seventy degrees one day, seventeen the next. Feeding continues for the cows and the mares only. The irrigation-system work winds down some.

April means the first of the annual rituals of spring in the burning of pastures, a task the Hubbards try never to undertake before mid-month. Sharon and Alan's Rule of Thumb: "If your pasture doesn't turn green in four days, you've burned too early." Meantime, foaling ends for Alan and lambing, at long last, for Joseph. Sharon spends the better part—some of the truly great parts—of her April days among the mares, checking and rechecking, feeling along with the moms, knowing them and their whinnied natures. Next year, the Hubbards plan to foal twenty mares, down from the forty they will bring to delivery this year.

Mares and stallions alike go out to summer grass in May. The custom cows come to graze, but this year, the family is down to just two clients, so much leased land lost to the encroachment coming north out of Manhattan, hilltop by hilltop, break by break, the ranchettes taking precious acreages an eighty at a time, the hunters buying land outright for their sport or securing exclusive leases so lucrative to the landowners that they prohibit grazing outright. Alan swings his left arm in a semicircle and says, "I'm aware of fifteen thousand acres right around where we're sitting that are now standing empty. Ground lost to hunting and urbanization." The Hubbards will cut hay this month, taking three cuttings before autumn, and grazing a fourth. "We get way more grazing days off alfalfa than with fertilized brome," says Sharon, who, because of careful movement of her horses, worries not at

Shannon Creek horses have built a reputation for breeding matched to the job at hand.

all about their bloating on a rich diet. "We're putting up what little brome hay we have," Alan says. "Mostly whatever we can find in the waterways and road ditches." This summer, as in the past few years, the Hubbards are running their own first-calf heifers as they work toward a cow herd planned to top out at 250.

Preparations for the horse sale have begun in July as hours of pasture time accumulate. Into the pastures to observe with precision and analysis and all appropriate memory, to make a mental or lead pencil note about the behavior of a cow, the look of a yearling, almost all of these observations coming from the back of a Shannon Creek colt, being readied for sales in a few weeks. All artificial insemination of June-calving Hubbard cows occurs in August. Foaling is full-blown, with still more work on the upcoming sale, more photography of horses as Sharon prepares the footnotes that will distinguish each one of the animals for potential buyers. A saddle on the photographed horse tells the buyer that the colt is broke to ride.

The sale catalog insists that "we continue to challenge our program with each new generation." The Hubbards' horses go to essentially four markets: ranchers, performers in the arena, young competitors and trail-ride operators needing horses suitable for families. "Our prospects are ranch raised in the Kansas Flint Hills, and the saddle horses had been started with a solid foundation, including miles of riding in big rugged pastures, learning from their mothers how to cross creek, travel rocky terrain and run in the hills. They have been pastured with cattle, sheep and goats." Fifty years into the family's quarter-horse breeding program, Sharon points to foundation broodmares as its great strength. "They're just beautiful matrons with size, big hips and good feet. They have a wonderful disposition, user-friendly in every way."

Sale day in late September brings three to four hundred people to the Manhattan Commission building, "standing room only" per a proud Alan, who has taken a full month's leave from the KSU dairy barn so that he can concentrate on the upcoming payday. Dozens of other potential buyers wait on phone lines and Internet connections. The 2013 Shannon Creek sale brought a buyer from Italy and another from New Zealand. In past years, these horses have sold into Russia, northern Europe, several into Mexico and many, many to a dude ranch in Wyoming, the ranch's owners flat sold on their disposition, just right for inexperienced riders up for the first time in rough country. "Some of our horses are just a little ranker though," Joseph says. "I'm thinking, for instance, of a dun gelding that will make a good ranch horse, but would never ever be suitable for a dude ranch."

Then, the hoopla of the big day past, with post-sale celebrations, naps and a half-day or two of doing absolutely nothing at all complete, the Hubbards turn to delivery of horses and cattle sold with all attending paperwork. The custom-grazed cattle are shipping, and Joseph is selling lambs, lots of lambs and goats, 90 percent of ram lambs sold directly to restaurants. Heritage Foods in New York has become a prime Hubbard customer, going so far as to send client chefs to Olsburg, Kansas, to learn about the lambs' production. Irrigation-pivot work begins once more, as the custom cows leave the ranch in October's last week. Broodmares, sorted by age, go to their winter ranges in November, and June-calving cows are maintaining maternal weight on corn stalks.

Now, with winter settling in, the feeding regimen imposes once more its monkish constraints, its all-day, all-night demands on the time and energy of an entire family. Once more, the Hubbards give themselves over to the hour-to-hour needs of the animals in their care.

Just as the sign says.

Cheryl

The classified advertisement in the *Kansas City Star* was straightforward enough: "Seamstress Wanted." She met the advertiser, appropriately enough, at a bar called Houlihans. He wanted a skilled person to make kilts, lots of them, made-to-order, of quality sufficient to make silly the continued importation of the garments from the British Isles.

And so, she would pick up the fabric and the measurements and begin to sew. Kilts are peculiar garments, requiring exact measurements at key points of the middle anatomy: waist, hip, ledge of hip and total length from belly button to the top of the knee. A uniquely personal garment for a quarrelsome people, the Scots, eventually forbidden to wear the tartans under pain of death, tartan the only fabric ever identifiable to a country, peculiar to a people who just love to fight.

She taught three neighbors the art of kilt making. Now these mothers are earning extra income from home, each working in her direct employ, and together the four of them ship two thousand kilts a year out of rural Eskridge, Kansas, as they have done for fifteen years and counting. Eskridge, at the eastern edge of the hills, where one long-ago autumn evening, she wore a crown above a corsage and a new dress, and she rode on the trunk of a convertible, and she waved to football bleachers full of people who knew her and cared about her.

This day she bears the slight scars of red-meat cookery. She volunteers every other Tuesday evening to cook a nice meal for the bingo players at the VFW Hall in Scranton, nine miles over. Two nights ago, in the midst of a contentious political debate in the kitchen, she absentmindedly threw some peppers into overheated grease, and the splatter blotched her high, perfect cheeks, pinprick burns here and there.

The kilts have now for the most part consumed two of her ten-year plans—sets of broad decisions, landmarks showing where she'd like to be, what she'd like to be doing on down the road. "I'm in a room sewing," she says. "I see myself in a room sewing."

The original rooster arrived already named Casserole. She named Casserole's first wife Mary Margaret. Their first male issue was Chick, of course, and there followed, in no particular order, Minnie, Henry and Justine. Four chicks bounce and yelp this day in a large box close to the fireplace in the living room.

She has become, by her own admission, "a celebrity with the burn…a crazy lady, because for the first couple of years I burned by myself." Her quarter-

Ingenious, willing and capable, Flint Hills families make all the best use of whatever resources are theirs.

section set on fire when the wind seemed to be right, a backfire set to protect the hay meadow to her south, its absentee owner not really in the picture. In her second year of one-on-one pyromania, her pasture fire damaged her cheese house, the little outbuilding where she stores her fresh cheeses, intended for sale at nearby farmers' markets. Built to code, the house and its certain sinks, its regulatory doors will serve as a workable metaphor.

She pursued the idle suggestion of a German lady to its illogical end. She makes ricotta and mozzarella and sour-cream-like quark as statements of the possible.

Thinking of a goat herd, the nannies' glorious milk, she lives alone, and she cheeses and she sews, listening as always she has for a whisper in the whirlwind.

A deadline waits. Ready now to press the pleats of an Irish kilt, a tartan named "saffron," a solid color, muted, not a plaid in sight. Lots of fabric involved in these fifty-four-inch hips, this forty-seven-inch waist, made for a woman to wear at a ceremonial gathering of clannish family. Six hours she put into this kilt, retailing now at $450, and she smiles on her way out the door, off in her pickup to meet the FedEx man. Self-contained and satisfied with the progress of the current, fifth ten-year strategy, alone in a world of her own making, splattered in the scalding oil of local religion, this anonymous, exquisite woman sews.

And in the thousand practiced, perfect stitches of this holy hour, perhaps too—this long-range believer, this homecoming queen—she dreams.

The Sylvesters

Andrew Sylvester grew up on a diversified farming operation—crops, cattle and hogs—east of Wamego. He worked hard through high school and excelled in his animal science studies at K-State where he traveled the countryside as a member of the university's livestock judging team. He married a hometown sweetheart, started a business offering highly specialized—unique, in fact—services in the backgrounding of bulls. Last summer, four generations of his family helped at harvest time, the Sylvesters working together as they always have.

The story is told of his grandfather working as a little boy with his brothers on the edge of Fort Riley at the extreme edge of the law. They were baling hay. They had cut the grass on the bombing range, and now they were using their newfangled J.I. Case field pickup baler, bouncing along on the trailer where, amid the dust and the gnats and the flying flecks of Sudan grass, he helped to stack the bales. The military police appeared on the scene of the Sylvesters' haying operation, where the brothers were promptly arrested for criminal trespassing, no one having told them that this grass happened to be the sole property of the United States government, not meant for diversion to the wintertime feeding of the Sylvester herd back on the home place. Little Lyle beat the rap, however, by hiding under the baler as the MPs rounded up his outlaw siblings. As they were marched off to the brig to await their shamefaced parents' arrival, Lyle climbed up on the tractor and finished baling the field. The Sylvester boys were like that; so is Lyle Sylvester's grandson.

Andrew Sylvester, barely out of college, started a business for himself. He found a workable site, cleaned the place up and installed the waterers and other infrastructure necessary to the care of largish ranch animals. In the first year of Sylvester Bull Development, he ran two hundred bulls through his company; in five years, he was taking care of a thousand. He helped owners in their selection and breeding strategies, gearing them toward

Arden and Austin Sylvester, cowmen.

A new generation of youngsters learns the mysteries of these hills at the old schoolhouse on the Tallgrass Prairie National Park.

current production and marketing conditions, all at an affordable price. Andrew developed those bulls in the identification of genetically superior animals. He showed his customers a profitable alternative to growing their own bulls in a trap back of the barn. He took over the factoring of time, capital, land, labor, facilities, nutrition and animal health, managing every developmental contingency for his owners. He groomed and photographed and advertised those bulls going to sale. Andrew worked every day to give every bull at SBD good, steady, appropriate growth in preparation for the longest possible productive life. Andrew Sylvester developed big, healthy bulls ready to serve as highly active herd sires.

And he lost it all.

Well, he has a nest egg, some money set aside for his boys' own time at K-State, for the beginnings of a cow herd, but no more Sylvester Bull Development. In the years of the company's meteoric growth, he took on a partner, a guy who forced Andrew out of the business he built.

There is no bitterness though, not in this direct descendant of a man who harvested government hay with his brothers in jail. "My grandpa has a lot of wisdom," a humble Andrew says, and the wise old gentleman has counseled Andrew back to a family undertaking that has always persevered in the face of unwelcome change. The Sylvesters were forced off that first family ranch, eminent domain in the expansion of adjacent Fort Riley, and they picked up and settled east of Wamego to build a life that now includes Laura, Arden, Austin and a baby on the way. Shy Andrew at last worked up the nerve to ask Laura on a date during their time in Manhattan, and she has come back to the ranch, too. Laura runs a part-time day-care service in the Sylvester home to supplement a family income that now comes primarily from the Kansas Livestock Association.

While in that quiet but quite relentless way of his, accumulating some mighty fine heifers, Andrew works as director of marketing and promotions and as a field man for KLA. His position calls for all sorts of educating and communicating on behalf of the association, various breeds of cattle and their owners and cattlemen large and small, statewide. So week to week, Andrew is traveling Kansas, often serving as a ringman at seedstock sales, helping cowmen on the most important day of their ranch's year. He sells advertising for *Kansas Stockman*, KLA's glossy ten-times-yearly publication. Good gosh, Andrew also supports the Young Stockman Academy, himself an alumnus of this program wherein KLA is educating "masters of beef advocacy"—young ranchers who are informed about every stage of the beef industry, from the genetics of a calf's sire and dam to that animal's eventual appearance on a plate at Jess and Jim's in Kansas City. Young ranchers who understand the legislative process and government's policy-making influences, good and bad, on Kansas cattlemen. Young ranchers schooled in public speaking and communication in all its forms, who can represent all that is best about the cattle business and the remarkable people who constitute it.

Remarkable, like a little boy hiding under a baler. Like a family of five trying, in their lives and their livelihood, to do the next right thing.

VERN HOSLER

The people who know him would find it inconceivable that Vern Hosler might ever raise his voice. Mother Teresa shouted way more in her life than Vern Hosler ever will. Yet there is something about him that refuses to compromise, a set of obvious convictions that never get mentioned in the course of doing a job the right way, a job in which alternatives to the cowboy way will not be discussed. There are rules of conduct on horseback, and the rules do not bend, so the horse doesn't need to hear a misplaced word and neither do the cowboys riding up and behind. Vern Hosler might never open his mouth and still be, what you might call, fierce.

He has walked away from ranch life twice in his eighty or so years. He didn't have much choice either time. He didn't whine when he left. He didn't whoop when he came back.

He quit school when he was sixteen, feeling, as he says, "out of place" in a high school that was so much bigger than, and so different from, the one-room schoolhouse of his boyhood, where he'd ride either bareback on his mare or double up behind an older woman, a sixth grader, who'd come by his family's home east of Climax, Kansas, to pick up her buddy Vern. The year he decided not to be a sophomore, he went to cowboying full-time, even though he'd already traded away that little mare he'd broke himself, the horse he still claims "would have climbed a tree for me if I'd asked her." He traded that mare to a neighbor for an unbroken filly and fifteen bucks' difference. Vern rode his prize mare to the neighbor's house, pocketed three five-dollar bills, threw his saddle on the filly and bounced her home. As a horse trader, he was a pretty fair welder.

With a wife and a second child coming, Vern left the Kansas Flint Hills for the Boeing Military Airplane Company, sealing fuel cells in the wings

Even the smallest of old Flint Hills towns boasted some glorious architecture.

of the huge aircraft in the Wichita plant. He went right back to cowboying when he couldn't take factory work anymore, signing on with Denny Rausch up in Thrall. Vern did it all, did it all for $200 a month, and somehow he supported a family that had grown to four children. He doubled his pay when he hired on with the sale barn in Hominy, Oklahoma. Denny drove Vern down to his new job and told his employers that they had a top hand about to join them. Then six months later, while he was trying to shut off a propane tank in the middle of a rainstorm, a fallen power line threw Denny Rausch into a fence. That barbed wire stayed lit like a Las Vegas rodeo for five or six hours until a passing neighbor finally found his body.

A man loses a good friend or a good horse, and he learns a thing or two, and maybe he loses the need to talk loud. What was to be said, after all, when the hail took the brim right off J.B. Bowman's straw and dropped it square on his shoulders, the yearlings just off the train in Cassoday running hard against the wind? Ten feet away, Vern crouched under the fenders, thinking less about some cute remark, less about slack-jawed, fat-mouthed nonsense.

More about how he and a partner with half a hat were going to bring those cattle another dozen miles up the road.

Craig Miller

The gene pool runs maybe fifteen thousand years deep, cold and relentless in its demands for quick, evolutionarily aggressive adaptation. Some of them—Utah's Sulphur Spring herd for example—have been called "zoological treasures," linked directly to the primitive Iberian strain of the species.

Look at them: some with zebra piano-key legs, some with triple dorsal stripes, others with barred chests. Look again, and see perhaps the only domesticated animal on earth with the will and the wherewithal to revert to snot-blowing, dirt-pounding, blood-toothed, hard-hard-hooved wildness.

And damned if they didn't.

Left behind with the Spaniards completing their imagined conquest, the Comanche dwindling off toward disappearance, the distant silver mines playing out, the Buffalo Soldiers riding back to Leavenworth, these horses ran farther into the mountains, deeper into the deserts of the American West. A while later, more than a million of them were drafted into combat duty in World War I. Tens of thousands more became chicken feed and dog treats. And in the choke and gasp of the Great Depression, stories circulated in

Their ancestral home in the inter-mountain West replaced by the grasslands now, these horses have come to Kansas to die.

small Western towns of horses weighted with old tires to make pickings easier for the rendering trucks after hot rods had run the animals to exhaustion. For a long, desperate time, these creatures seemed to be following the bison off a killer cliff of their own untamed choosing.

First released in the seventeenth century to roam the high meadows, to reproduce along the ridges where a sentry always stood, these horses made their wild way across western North America for five centuries before the United States government decided to again get involved. The Wild Horse Annie Act of 1959 came first, and it must be said that this landmark legislation, as with the laws that followed, took hold in footing much more emotional than economic. As word of the wild horses' fight for survival spread across the nation, America's schoolchildren and their mothers put pen to paper. Deluged with outrage printed in pencil on Big Chief tablets in the largest letter-writing campaign on a nonwar issue in United States history, Congress passed in a unanimous vote the Wild Free-Roaming Horse Act of 1971, asserting that "wild horses and burros are living symbols of the historic and pioneer spirit of the West; that they contribute to the diversity of life forms within the Nation and enrich the lives of the American people, and that these horses and burros are fast disappearing from the American scene."

The law is the law, and the legislation had established, with no roaming room for argument, wild horses' "legal right to live on public lands," as the act suggested, "without harassment," although it must be said that anyone attempting to harass one of these chestnut mares a first time will most certainly not be bothering her again.

Ask Craig Miller of rural Cassoday, Kansas.

Tall, thick and lean at the same time in the mold of men who have done physical labor their entire lives, Craig describes being launched by a goofy one that decided a short ride in Craig's trailer was not really what he had in mind after all. With a dozen or so of his gelded brothers already safely aboard, this horse turned and kicked with NFL ferocity just as Craig was shutting the trailer gate. Suddenly twenty feet south, Craig shook himself to run and jump and roll from the mayhem he just knew was headed his way. But, you know, that horse was already past, some speed and some movement learned from Nevada lightning at play in a cowboy's spinning nightmare.

Craig rides the 777 Ranch where, as of February 2007, 4,487 wild horses roamed relatively free. The Bureau of Land Management sends veterinarians as needed, and Craig's work consists of receiving the newcomers and allotting the pastures and planning the movements and, most of all, feeding the horses through a Kansas winter.

Some of the locals question the wisdom of seven thousand acres of good grass and bunches of taxpayer money given over to a dead-end breed. But everyone likes soft-spoken, easy-to-grin Craig Miller. They admire his cowboy skills, his quiet integrity, his patience in the face of a life-altering change of responsibilities, the cattle gone in lieu of these helicoptered, starved-out, dry-mouthed, buckshot old nags.

And their fierce refusal to, like the lifestyle they would replace, die quietly.

GLASSEL FLAHERTY

Precious few people have witnessed the purposeful interference of man with nature, the climactic combination of genetics, electricity and male urge that is the extraction of bull semen. Even fewer people have participated, up close and wet and stinky, in this critical first step in the artificial insemination (AI) of high-value cows and heifers. If we're going

Bazaar, Kansas, Memorial Day, 2014.

to have a calf here in nine months, we're going to need some high-powered seed on the spot.

The GI Bill in his back pocket, Glassel Dane Flaherty took the AI course as a sophomore at the Kansas Artificial Breeding Service Unit (KABSU) in the college town of Manhattan, just down the road from Fort Riley, home of the army's First Division, the Big Red One. At graduation, he took a job as an AI technician, assisting in the lab in the evaluation and processing of the semen. In time, he became the lab manager and then took on the collecting tasks as well, using a teaser steer and artificial vaginas at the KABSU barn, relying on the electrode in the field. In either case, Glassel knew firsthand the throes of orgasmic bulls, their locomotive bellows, old boys of a ton and more whose eyes bulged in 270-degree peripheral vision of their first date with a 135-pound Irishman. Unruly farm animals did not stand a chance against Glassel Flaherty.

Neither did the Viet Cong.

November 17, 1967: Alpha Company of the Twelfth Infantry was pinned down there on Hill 1338 overlooking Dak To, the enemy above hunkered and fortified. But Glassel Flaherty and his friends were edging their way up, digging with their knees and their elbows, their noses deep in the protective earth, the machine guns and North Vietnamese Army rockets doing their worst, Glassel cranking the radio, calling in howitzer fire on the enemy above. Until, for reasons of his own, he lay down his radio pack, and he commenced his farm-boy assault on the People's Republic of Vietnam. He charged the first bunker in his typically direct way, emptying the clip from his M14, his left-handed grenades silencing these particular Vietnamese forever, he believed. Private First Class Flaherty then turned his attention, the hail and the wither of his aim, to a second bunker, going one-on-twenty until his buddies could finish the job, only seven in Alpha Company not killed or wounded in the battle.

In the arrival of his Bronze Star for Valor, the army in its roundabout way said he had "distinguished himself."

Later he lived, hour to hour, with the routine of a cloistered nun, the allotments of time necessary to get the work all done. He woke every morning of his adult life at three o'clock. He woke to the explosion of 104-millimeter rockets seeking their prey in the dark. Way before first light, Glassel heard again the murderous bursts of a machine-gun bunker that refused to shut the hell up.

On December 29, 2007, he stuck napkins up his nostrils to stop a nosebleed that in two days' time said acute myeloid leukemia, the bastard offspring of Agent Orange seeded all over the denuded hills where Alpha Company was sent to bleed. So he sucked up chemo by the barrel. A year later, he borrowed some bone marrow from a generous German he named "Hans," and then he went home to the farm to hang it up.

He died at 4:30 a.m.—Glassel Dane Flaherty, the artificial inseminator, the human alarm clock.

The hero.

PETE FERRELL

The dead cow hung without hope from gin poles rigged frontal on the 1953 civilian-issue Dodge Powerwagon, its engine cold and dead, the power-takeoff locked, an altogether tipsy little calculation underway between ditch-side equipoise and a thirty-foot tumble straight down into the dead pile, the bones of other blizzards, the bleached skulls of pneumonia waiting below.

The independent cowboy career of young Garland Peter Ferrell III had begun.

Some old boys find a piece of grass they enjoy, and they don't ever, ever leave. Jack Ferrell (nee Garland Peter Ferrell Jr.), Pete's dad, was that way, content to sit among his calvers, to ride the fence lines and come home after dark to Isabelle, whom he had brought to the highest point of the Flint Hills of Kansas, a place where Grouse, Rock, Hickory and Otter Creeks flow off to all points of the compass. Young Jack had first come to his own dad's ranch in 1918—strictly a summer place in those days, no cows wintered then—fleeing a nasty flu epidemic back home in Wichita, the old house heaving under the wind and the snow coming in. Jack, the youngest up on a steady bay horse; his dad, Garland Peter Ferrell; and his older siblings, they tromped through the white-out the seven miles into Beaumont and its hotel just across the tracks from the water tower.

Then, sixty-three years later, Jack away on his first real vacation ever, his first extended few days gone from the ranch to watch Nebraska beat LSU 17-10 in the Orange Bowl down in Florida, and Pete is left to look after the herd. A bad blizzard takes three head, and Pete and an old college buddy are out to bury the dead.

A determined, declared independence has informed Ferrell DNA for generations. Lloyd Bascombe Ferrell, Pete's great-grandfather, came west after leaving Virginia at sixteen years of age, both his parents killed in the Civil War. The first telegrapher in Council Grove, Kansas, L.B. Ferrell sold apples for a time just to make the rent. He bought residential lots in what would become Kansas's largest city and—a real-estate bust underway in Wichita—Mr. Bascombe Ferrell in 1888 tied some #9 wire around his waist, declared himself a cowboy and drove in a buggy fifty miles east to begin putting the ranch's seven thousand acres together, a quarter section at a time.

Old Jack, Pete's grandfather, hated the creeping communalism of the New Deal so much that he refused to cash his Social Security checks, so much so that the Ferrell Ranch, the creeks notwithstanding, is water poor to this day because of his refusal to share in the federally underwritten construction of "two-year ponds"—deep, well-designed waterholes capable of withstanding a thirty-month drought.

And so Pete came home from Grinnell College with a degree in cultural anthropology. (His dad had sent him there, considering the boy too rural for Harvard, from whence the previous two generations of Ferrell men had found their way into the world.) He came back to the ranch thinking of Zebulon Pike's description—from up on the site of present-day Hamilton, Kansas—of herds of bison a mile wide and three days in the passing by. Pete wonders why the same grass might not produce similar sorts of animal protein with somewhat less effort than that required by prevalent theories of ranch management. Pete has never, by any means, been averse to work—and he and manager Jamie Nelson care for the contract cattle grazing on the ranch as if they were his children—but to this day, he wonders about ear-tagging and calf-pulling, about vaccinations and force-feeding of toxic-rich rations in feedlots.

In yet another pursuit of a new way of ranching, Pete was one of nine cowboys sitting around the table at the formation of Tallgrass Beef, a ranchers' cooperative that sought to, at last, demonstrate the economic viability of finishing these Flint Hills steers on this Flint Hills grass, of sending cattle to market straight from the pasture. Three years later, a reefer full of hanging, grass-finished primo beef went warm—the power off, all thawed then and ruined even for lion food—and Tallgrass Beef watched its future run to dirt like the dark blood dripping from that failed freezer.

And you know, in situational irony not lost on Pete Ferrell, it was electricity that killed the co-op.

The towers are visible from forty miles, unearthly in their Cape Kennedy rise from the prairie, and he understood full well the whirlwind of neighborly opposition to come when first he thought to build electrical generators on his ranch.

The Kansas chapter of the Sierra Club, in a position paper of January 2003, minced few words in its endorsement of the development of wind energy in cow country. "It is our opinion that all areas of Kansas should be open to development provided proper safeguards are taken to ensure environmental impacts are marginal. This is a clean, renewable source of electricity generation which can significantly reduce our dependence on fossil fuels, especially coal, a major source of green gasses and other pollutants. Furthermore, wind energy can help preserve precious resources such as natural gas and help limit the further development of nuclear energy." To which Pete Ferrell adds, "Wind energy is just another way to sustain agriculture in these hills. It's a resource as much as this bluestem grass."

The Flint Hills Tallgrass Prairie Heritage Foundation had other ideas. Formed with a dozen additional big objectives in mind, the FHTPHF in its fourteenth purpose came obliquely to the point: "to promote implementation of siting guidelines for industrial wind turbine commercial electrical power generation facilities which are ecologically sophisticated, environmentally responsible, socially relevant, and economically rational and will not impose upon the unique national and international natural resource treasure that is the Flint Hills Tallgrass Prairie ecosystem."

Tall as a 747 jetliner stood on its nose, the turbines south of Beaumont are visible north of Eureka, forty miles and more, as the wind blows.

Whew.

The complaint stretched across almost two hundred pages, and all the verbiage reduced to "Pete, your turbines are ugly." With a coalition of ranchers, conservationists and wildlife enthusiasts filing a federal lawsuit to halt development of the Elk River Windfarm, this $190 million project involving an even one hundred generating towers to be constructed for the most part on the Ferrell Ranch and a few more towers across the road on the late Les Cooper's grass.

It came down then to a three-to-two county-commission vote in favor of the wind farm for these reasons, and these alone: increased tourism, the privately financed improvement in roads, the project's consistency with the county's planning and zoning prospectus, the creation of jobs, its overall safety and—get this—its effect on the view.

And here's the agricultural upshot: no change whatsoever in grazing patterns, and no birds, not one, killed by the propellers (as documented by researchers from Kansas State University); the Flint Hills changed all right, but as one neighbor says, "Those things aren't near as bad as I thought they'd be." Manager Nelson talks of cattle lined up on a hot afternoon, enjoying the shade of the towers, easing along as the shadows edge east to west and back again. Still, one of Ferrell's erstwhile partners in Tallgrass Beef once walked up to him, called him the devil, and announced that those infernal towers would ruin the Flint Hills forever.

It could have gone either way: one, the mama cow's dead weight might have pulled the Dodge Powerwagon into the pit, or two, the engine might have started at last and, with the winch released and the cadaver deposited below, Pete and his buddy might have driven away, his dad none the wiser.

Pete Ferrell found a third option.

With the truck chained to a tree, Pete took a limb saw, climbed out onto the gin poles and cut the poor animal's front legs free. Voila! The chain removed, Pete watched the Powerwagon slip, for no particular reason at all, straight over the cliff.

With nontraditional ways to sustain ranching in these parts as with cleaning up after a blizzard, one never knows for sure. An old boy just never really knows.

THE DUNAFONS

Wayne Dunafon's dad told him, "If you don't want to walk, break a horse." Clarence Dunafon knew whereof he spoke. He trained horses, and he urged his son to follow in his business of teaching manners to unruly farm animals. Young Wayne Dunafon learned well the hardscrabble lessons of hard times among hard, hard-loving people.

He was born in 1919 in Yuma, Colorado, was potty trained in the Sand Hills of western Nebraska, rocked around in the horse-drawn wagon that took his family to Russell, Kansas, when he was five years old. Where Russell, like every other small town in Kansas, felt the brunt of Dust Bowl winds, the gnaw of a collapsing rural economy, Clarence worked on a little spread he had leveraged to the hilt. He broke horses for the neighbors. He planted a few crops. He tried every agricultural means of making any money at all. But then the hogs died of cholera, the cattle of malnutrition—no feed for the animals and not so much for the Dunafons. Wayne's mom, Jessie, a rugged woman of resilience and quiet strength, hung wet sheets on the open windows to let a little breeze into a sweltering house. Next morning, Jessie took down those sheets, now weighing a solid ten pounds, mudded up in dirt that came from somewhere down in Oklahoma. His dad worked on, but finally he just could tolerate the drudgery and the loss no more. His natural nomadism kicked in, and Clarence Dunafon took his family back to Colorado, just when Wayne was making himself known thereabouts as a football player, the scholarship offers already arriving in his junior year. But Wayne knew he could rodeo in Colorado just as he had in Kansas, participating in five events by the age of eighteen, already a pro and a member of the Cowboy Turtles Association, Wayne ready for the assorted mayhem each of those five events threw at him.

At twenty-one, he came back to Kansas on a Riss Company potato truck, the ride in exchange for unloading several tons of root vegetables. He moved to Westmoreland, Kansas, with, as he used to say, "seven dollars and a saddle." The little town became the base of operations for a rodeo hand out on the circuit, the rough-stock and timed events coming naturally to a young man who had grown up around horses. He rode with the great ones, with Gerald Roberts and Casey Tibbs and Jim Shoulders. He and Gerald carried on the friendliest of personal competitions, most particularly with a horse named Schoolboy Rowe, after the great Detroit Tigers pitcher. Legend has it that Wayne rode Schoolboy four times, while the stalwart Roberts never could. The story continues that Wayne's dad, who was trying to promote

Schoolboy as unrideable, asked Wayne to allow himself to be bucked off. "Not even for you, Dad," came the reply, and a horse who sent flying—legend says—more than four hundred cowboys, whose favorite trick was to come straight over backward to the rodeo dirt...well, he turned out to be rideable after all. "He had a different style of bucking," Wayne would say. "If you pulled on his head at all, he would rear up and fall over on you." That horse would try to kill you outright, just like plastering a man with his mouth full.

The *Onaga Herald* of November 13, 1930, headlined this story, "Fred O'Daniel Fatally Shot," and then, in the purplish journalistic prose of the time, recounted the details:

> *One of the most atrocious and coldblooded crimes in the history of this county took place last Tuesday evening about 7:30 o'clock, when Fred O'Daniel, county commissioner from the first district, was shot and instantly killed at his beautiful farm home, just south of Westmoreland. Mr. O'Daniel was sitting at the supper table with his family when the shot was fired, the bullet entering through a screened-in porch, a window pane, and penetrating his skull. Mr. O'Daniel has served the county for nearly eight years as commissioner and was well liked by everyone. No motive for such a crime can be imagined, although at this time, county officers say that they are working on several clues which may lead to the arrest of the guilty party.*

Mrs. O'Daniel moved out of that house and refused to come back to it.

Ten years later, Wayne Dunafon walked into the bank in Westmoreland, asking for a loan to buy equipment sufficient to working his bottom acreage, and the banker came back with an offer of, "Why not use Fred O'Daniel's equipment? It's yours to use, if you'll just live in that fine, old house and look after it for a time." So Wayne moved into the deserted mansion's kitchen, lived in that one room among the twenty-two under the roof and stayed there a year in peace with the ghost of a fine county commissioner, whose cattle drives to the railhead at St. George on the Kaw River would begin up north of Flush and end with a thousand head and more after the gatherings along the ten-mile drive.

Before his thirtieth birthday, Wayne had ridden and roped and wrestled himself into a ranking among the top-ten all-around rodeo cowboys in the world, and soon he would add two all-around championship saddles to his trophy room out in the barn. In 1956, he was runner-up bulldogger in the Professional Rodeo Cowboy Association championships. At the Gladwater

Round-Up down in Texas, Wayne bulldogged a steer in 2.9 seconds. That sort of speed and strength unheard of, Wayne roared out of the box, dropping down into the groove with his arms already around the animal's horns, his feet planted, the twist of the steer's head and down on into county-fair glory.

His largest purse ever amounted to four thousand dollars, twice—one for placing third in Madison Square Garden and the other for third in the Boston Garden. Still, all the winnings that came home went to the savings account, principal and a little interest intended for the acquisition of countryside. The first three-hundred-acre parcel, along with the ongoing trust of a banker in Manhattan, came in 1940, a spread with a two-story frame house so rickety that the wind rippled the linoleum. Not much of a place to bring an exotic star of Broadway musicals, a young woman used to Park Avenue restaurants and million-dollar apartments on the Upper West Side. Wayne's twenty-one-year-old wife stayed with him three years in that house with no electricity, a pitcher pump for water and maybe the first outhouse that mighty fancy lady had ever seen. In those three years, Wayne continued to rodeo, continued to win and continued to buy land, to buy it by any means at his disposal. Enter the Black-Market Sausage King of the Lower East Side, Mr. Karl Mueller. This friend of his wife's family was stuffing his walls with cash made from illegal Wiener schnitzel, the beef used therein supposed to be reserved for the troops in that first year of America's involvement in World War II. On the flight back home, the wadded up cash was falling out of the borrowed suit too tight on a Kansas cowboy. Wayne brought that money of questionable origin but wholesome intent back to Mr. Sam Sidebottom of rural Potawatomie, Kansas, to whom he paid thirty-five dollars for each of eighty stout, spring-fed acres. Let it be known that Wayne Dunafon returned, with 1 percent interest, every dime of Karl Mueller's money, as the note on lined yellow paper said he would.

In 1951, the romance had gone out of the rodeo, and the somewhat wifely Suzanne bailed. With her, she took her ownership in exactly half of her ex-husband's hard, hard-earned land. But the thoughtful (some might say wily) Wayne decided which half. And besides—what's the difference to a snot-nosed actress between nasty Kansas land with water and that nasty Kansas land without water. So he gave her in the divorce settlement the land along Rock Creek, its lying name no cover for the mudded-up flow of its rainy days, nor the name any description of its silted bottom, all too obvious in the much more frequent days of its dryness. And Wayne kept the land surrounding Wilson Creek and its feeding, nurturing springs, the stream never dry, always good fresh water for thirsty steers off grass that could hide their bottom half.

Then in 1956, while flying Braniff, Wayne Dunafon met a woman: just twenty-one years of age, beauteous and strong willed, but sweet, sweet beyond a cowboy's ability to say, Miss Lori Ferguson of 5804 North Manton Avenue, Chicago, northwest side. Lori had lost her father when she was but two years of age; her stepfather died when she was eleven. And she learned the sort of independence that made her an airline stewardess at eighteen, in a time when women were still rare in the workforce. Maybe he—on July 10, 1958, their wedding day—was ready to be tamed. Maybe his Lori was simply too much woman to ever, ever leave, even for just a weekend's romp on some broncs. No matter. Immediately, she began to travel with him, and when Doug came along, he too among the hands behind the chutes at Cheyenne and down in Amarillo. His mother says, "We have a picture of him in his cowboy clothes with a hat and boots, and some rodeo rider put a cigarette in his mouth for the photograph." Doug, like his father, was not a smoker at the time.

Wayne's mom helped Lori make the old windblown house a home. "Wayne had no money for such things; all his winnings went into buying land and machinery. I had saved $1,600 from my time as a stewardess, and Wayne's mom took us to Kansas City and we bought enough furniture for the kitchen, the living room and our bedroom." Lori Dunafon was a pioneer woman for sure; she put the product of her labors into the nurturing of the two men in her life—and, soon enough, a daughter, Wendy—and she found in their care the stuff of her greatness. To this day, she slides about with raisin-cream pie and lemonade, with the strength of memory of an exceptionally bright teenager, with both maternal and extracurricular joys sufficient to the gladdening of a small town.

There was a time though when she had to share her Wayne with a reading, watching world. Once, up in Wyoming, she stood outside the cameras of a screen test for a cowboy to appear in advertisements for Marlboro cigarettes. Wayne came to the rescue of a hapless Chicago ad agency that had earlier chosen a pretty-boy male model who put on cowboy clothes and walked into the ads wearing his spurs upside down. When hooting letters arrived at Phillip Morris headquarters, the agency decided only real cowboys would do. And so came the interviews at Cheyenne Frontier Days.

For fourteen years, from 1964 to 1978, he rode the range as the Marlboro Man. Wayne Dunafon earned in one day—$350—a working cowboy's monthly pay. But he earned every penny, projecting an unmistakable realism as a man doing little more than being himself. The photographers worked him hard though, Wayne loping the agency's wrangled horses through action shot after action shot. Wayne used to say that "they'd take ten thousand photos in three days and then be happy if they got a half-dozen magazine ads out of it." Once, out in Wyoming on a wintertime shoot, the horses and cowboys and camera crews had to be plowed out of the deep, accumulating snow—but what magnificent shots in the weeklong meantime. Only once, just outside Strong City, did the Chicago creative directors find the Flint Hills sufficiently western for a Marlboro backdrop, and so Wayne traveled from Texas to Oregon, saddled up and waiting for some photographer to yell, "Action!"

Wayne's weathered face and steer-wrestling build made him the macho icon of Lee Rider jeans, Firestone tires and Chevy pickups as well.

But before, after and through it all, he ranched. Those driven by agenda will insist that he died of lung cancer, a charge false in every way. Wayne Dunafon passed from causes entirely natural at the age of eighty-two. And four years after his death, old Wayne found his cowboy way to Oklahoma City and the National Cowboy Hall of Fame.

His son looks back on his time on the ranch: "I got to work with my dad every day for eleven years in a cow-calf operation that let us both cowboy to our heart's content, and then I decided I wanted to try my hand in construction." So he came off the cow herd and began building houses, and now he's developing an eighty-lot subdivision north of Wamego called Brookridge.

Doug comes home to a treehouse. He and his wife, Vicki, have built a spectacular house on the edge of a ridge (what amounts to a cliff in these hills), and his living room looks out over the tops of hundred-year-old oaks. A quarter mile into the trees run the unmistakable ruts of the Oregon Trail. He remembers again the old place, now turned in on itself, as glaciated as the hills that surround it, dead of its own weight, frozen now in the generalities of decline, only the cypress used up in the soffets still whole and recognizable in its original intent. He mowed the grass there in what he calls "the best boyhood a kid could have."

Doug drives along an alfalfa field not reseeded for a dozen years. It stands preblue, ready for yet another cutting, six this year. He has opinions about such fields: "Sure, it sits on bottom ground along a creek that doesn't go dry, and its roots stretch ten feet deep. But too many people wait too long to cut their alfalfa. They worry too much about the weather forecast. Cut the damned stuff. It'll dry out."

The Dunafons made a home here, and then time came and changed it all.

Not a waterpark in the world can match Dunafon Beach for family fun.

Son Justin and a buddy have begun a firewood endeavor, Vicki the filer of papers necessary to a proper, legal, recognized business. The boys have taken to the work with the exuberance of youth, the forethought of genuine agricultural entrepreneurism. Silent partner Doug takes a 10 percent cut for the youngsters' use of his handmade log splitter and his vehicles, which cost them $0.56 per mile. The giant front loader with the shear and the grapple comes at no charge, borrowed for a while from the construction business, but Dad picks the trees for removal, their disappearance part of a thoughtful clearing plan that leaves free for the picking up any forest products on the ground. Homeowners in Manhattan will find the bundles of oak and hackberry and elm a bargain at $3.25 a bundle, and the boys clear $500 hard cash plus lessons in work and capitalism absolutely priceless in their lifelong application.

Only a sophomore, Justin Dunafon looks to score big in a Future Farmers of America competition—his firewood deal a seeming winner on three strong points: it benefits agriculture in the removal of unwanted trees (one), which becomes a source of green energy (two) in a youthful venture that is entrepreneurial all the way (three).

Doug and Justin have planted a thirty-five-foot pole on an island they made in a pond they purposely drew down just for fun. Just for fun this ranch-made hoodedoo, an old rusted grain bin with an eighteen-foot diameter sunk ten feet onto a rock platform that father and son built to level the binned island with deep water all around, perfect for diving and dropping from the rope swing to be swiveled from the top of the pole, a take-off deck to be constructed at pond's edge, some high-school trigonometry in practical application with the height of that deck, that pole and the length of that rope.

Miss Lori Ferguson Dunafon of rural Potawatomie County will sit there this summer, up from that pond, and she will listen to the hoots and squeals of her grandchildren, and she will think of her Wayne and how he used to say, "Sure, I rodeoed a lot, but what else could you do back then and make so much money while having such a good time?"

Just released from a rope, upside down above deep clear water, another generation of Dunafons will learn again that good fun and good money almost always come in the company of good family.

Jake Betts

He fit the loose physical, mental and moral requisites for ceremonial guard duty, including functions at the White House, the Pentagon and the Tomb of the Unknown Soldier, and he understood the sheer, overwhelming honor of it all. But representing the United States Marine Corps in this nation's military's most solemn observances was not exactly the reason why he had joined up. Jake Betts became a marine to fight in Iraq. "I was young. It was the right thing to do," he says with easy matter-of-factness, the job done now.

Not that the selection process for the Corps' Honor Guard advanced with much other than the usual "Shut up, and do as you're told" procedural mentality of boot camp anyway. "Guys with a thirty-inch waist right here." "Six foot or so? Right here too." "Arrest record—you're out of here!" "Drugs, ditto!"

"Are you in debt, recruit?" a drill instructor screamed at Jake. "No, sir! 1991 Ford 150 pickup, paid for, sir!" The drill instructor laughed, and Jake found himself to be, in his employer's opinion, a squared-away individual deserving of wearing the Marine Corps dress uniform for presidential and Pentagon events, for wreath layings at the Tomb. He took his responsibilities seriously, and he looked good, real good, on command. But the two years of living ceremoniously dragged by, until at last he escaped his non-deployable unit at the Marine Barracks, Eighth and I Streets, down by the Washington Navy Yard. He humped it on back to First Battalion, First Marines, his platoon sergeant back in D.C. having recommended him for sniper platoon selection.

The overseers of the sniper selection process "worked my fanny off. They didn't let you eat much. Didn't let you sleep much. Anything to try to make a guy quit." By the end of it all, "I was sore everywhere." But he was in peak physical condition, had earned an expert medal in marksmanship back in boot camp and suddenly was in a platoon to learn to kill from a distance, mastering mission planning, optics, ballistics, stalking and, always, more marksmanship. At last, he deployed with First Battalion, First Marines, Scout Sniper Platoon, Blackheart Seven, a marine infantryman with special shooting skills, and he came to Al-Karmah outside of Fallujah, Iraq, in 2006, at a genuinely bad time in that city's history. Some shrapnel burned into his hip and one of his thighs just outside of town, and he rotated with his unit back to the states with a Purple Heart on his chest.

Decision time—back to combat or back to cowboying. Miss Amy would have something to do with the decision. Pretty and smart and, like him,

Jake Betts, cowboy.

devout and knowledgeable in the following of the Bible's teachings, this Kentucky girl found her cowboy down in Texas. They married while his dress blues were still around in the nation's capital.

He had grown up in Caney, Kansas, down on the Oklahoma border where the Flint Hills taper into the Osage country. "My folks gave me a horse instead of a television," he says, and that one gift has made all the difference. He went everywhere on Dandy, most of all the seven miles to meet his cousin Jess coming seven miles from the other way across Montgomery County. He didn't ride with a saddle until years of bareback had taught him the nuances of controlling a horse. On a day second only to meeting Amy, he met Red Davis, a cowboy of the old school, badly bowlegged, half Seneca Cayuga, "the greatest cowboy that ever lived," in Jake Betts's mind, a man who showed him skills with a rope like unto his horsemanship, and right there, you had yourself a hand.

Jake moved to Howard, Kansas, to work for John Cannon. John's dad, Harry, was an old rodeoing buddy of Red's. His cowboy education continued with the Cannons. He took to caring for yearlings on grass, and he just couldn't get enough of the life. He dreamed of the big spreads, and he made the ranch rodeos down in Texas, asking managers if maybe they could use a young cowboy with some try in him. He worked a short time on the Pitchfork in the fall of 1997 before coming back to the Cannon spread. Then he took off for northern Arizona and the Diamond A and the old ways there, the chuck wagon and the jigger boss and the multiple horses per cowboy, all on a ranch exceeding eight hundred thousand acres of wild country leased from the Navajo reservation. "Nobody, except maybe the manager, knows how big that ranch is," says Jake, of those flyover places by Seligman.

He was allowed by that manager to ride a horse, and he showed the man what he could do, the way he intended to work around here. Then, out onto the lonesome with the wagon on the toughest horse he ever bridled, a Diamond A traveler, and "there was just no bottom to him. He'd go and go some more." And always the rituals, the right and true cowboy ways of the old-timers: every morning the wrangler would bring the horses necessary for a day's work on the hard side of things, the houlihans flying out there thirty feet and more; the quiet working of a morning's chosen horse to get any buck out of him right here and now; the silent trot behind the wagon boss out of camp, a snake of cowhands following him through the dropping of cowboys at their starting spots, the gathering of cattle in rough country a straight-ahead proposition, through the brush and never, ever around it,

The pastures in Jake Betts's care stretch for miles, places where a man might think of final things.

just men and horses with no trucks, no trailers and no fences—all for $650 a month, the use of eight assigned horses, every meal outside and, with luck, a soap shower about every ten days.

And always the straight ahead, never the roundabout. "There were no horses spinning in circles; they'd fire you for that. You were paid to bring wild cattle out of the brush. You rode right through it." To this day, he wears chaps tough enough to whip Russia.

He had lived a young cowboy's perfect life or, better, a young, unmarried cowboy's life. And so, mustered out at Camp Pendleton, Jake brought Amy back to Kansas, to its smaller pastures, to a place where a man might be a good cowboy and a good husband all in the same day. "I'd always liked the grass in this country," Jake says from the living room, two houses south of the Bazaar Schoolhouse. In an old place he's fixing up, with Amy making it home, he's looking after cattle and shoeing horses.

He's also studying—studying hard with a Bible college out of Southlake, Texas, and his work with the yearlings comes before nights in the preparation of a paper on "a more comprehensive, more focused understanding of Paul's comments in Romans 1:16," wherein Jake is exploring, in particular, "the disciple's assertion, 'I'm not ashamed of the gospel.'" He does not intend to join the ministry, content to be a teacher in his church, Flint Hills Community, in Cottonwood Falls.

Jake did not come directly to this happy place in his life.

Cliff Cole is a manager of the Range Management Group of National Farms, based in Cottonwood Falls, and he saw what he had in Jake Betts. After USMC-sponsored farrier school in Missouri and crisscrossing the hills in Morris, Chase and Greenwood Counties, Jake had found no one with stable, ongoing work for a cowhand of the first rank. No one but Cliff Cole, and "he gave me a chance. Cliff gave me a start into this country, and I'm grateful for it."

A thousand miles from nowhere, gratitude comes like the rain. Hard and certain, just before and after it absolutely must have to happen.

The Land: Its Own High-Priced Self

Mr. Cole is a fine judge of cattle, of men and of land. In January 2007, *Beef* magazine printed its assessment of the price of pasture in the Flint Hills, the record-high going rates for grass back then bringing in a new wave of outside ownership.

The specific occasion for the magazine's look: the October 2006 sale at auction of the historic Rogler Ranch north of Matfield Green, a spectacular piece of Kansas—4,081 acres grown from the homesteaded, 160 acres belonging to Austrian immigrant Charles Rogler, who walked all the way from Iowa to stake his claim. Sold in seven separate tracts at an average price of $1,696 per acre—a total of $6.92 million—the ranch found itself with new owners, only one of whom was involved in the cattle business. The other buyers came from far away, an insurance executive from Maryland, for example, an oil-and-gas family from Texas, a group of investors from Illinois. Together, they represented in exact terms the arrival of huge amounts of capital that were pushing land prices to record highs, inflation be damned. As the article noted, however, a regular buyer of available ranch land did not come away with any Rogler acreage.

> *Conspicuously absent from the Rogler sale was Texas billionaire Edward Bass, whose Texas and Kansas ranchland holdings include 33,123 acres in Chase County. A portion of Bass's spread adjoins the Rogler Ranch.*

"Our viewpoint is that pasture prices are obviously too high," says Cliff Cole, Bass's local ranch manager in Cottonwood Falls, KS. Bass last added to his Flint Hills holdings in spring 2005, when he paid $920/acre for 1,220 acres just east of the Rogler Ranch. The price was a new area high at the time.

A month later, in early February 2007, the 7,317-acre Dunne ranch in Butler County, thirty miles south, sold for $1,055, just as predicted by Joe Sundgren, the auctioneer from El Dorado, Kansas, who oversaw the ranch's sale. Joe had predicted a sale price of $700 to $1,500 per acre, and the middle-ground actual price bore out the enduring value of solid bluestem grass even if the wide-open Dunne spread lacked the old architecture and colorful history of the Rogler ranch.

Today, Joe looks out at that grass and finds comfort in its quality. "The new owners here were all cattle people. They're taking care of the grass. There's no grubbing going on around here." That said, he has watched land prices climb even higher, as several recent listings at Sundgren Realty suggest:

240+- ACRES BUTLER COUNTY, KS LAND TUESDAY APRIL 15, 2014 6:00 P.M.
SOLD for $2800/acre!! Excellent Tract Of Native Flint Hills Pasture With A Watershed Lake, A Large Pond, And Great Access.
160+- ACRES BUTLER COUNTY, KS LAND WEDNESDAY MARCH 26, 2014 6:00 P.M.
SOLD for $320,000! That's $2,000/acre! Excellent Combination of Kansas Bluestem Pasture, Tillable Ground, and Brome Grass with Two Ponds, an Old Windmill, and Pipe Livestock Pens. Located South of Leon, KS and Just ½ Mile From Blacktop.

But then, Joe Sundgren looks northwest twenty miles from his office, and he remembers a sale five months ago in which farm ground asserted its value—as opposed to good grass over all that flint and limestone rock.

80+- ACRES BUTLER COUNTY, KS LAND THURSDAY FEBRUARY 20, 2014 6:00 P.M.
SOLD for $472,000! That's $5900/acre! Excellent Tillable Ground North of Whitewater, Kansas. Great Location and Excellent Access. Blacktop Frontage Along the West Boundary and a Hedge Row Along the South.

Every auction these days brings with it ripple effects on neighboring landowners and often on the cattlemen who lease land thereabouts.

And then, the total package, as Sundgren Realty's sales blurb notes:

> *320+- ACRES BUTLER COUNTY, KS LAND THURSDAY FEBRUARY 13, 2014 6:00 P.M.*
> *SOLD for $976,000! That's $3050/acre! Native Flint Hills Pasture, Creek, Tillable, Part of a Watershed Lake, Timber, Oil Production, and Ponds. Very Rarely Will You Find Flint Hills Land With a Better Combination of Agriculture, Hunting, Fishing, Recreation, & Income.*

But Sundgren Realty's biggest sale in recent memory came in the context of a truck driver. Frank Bills was his name, and he started his working life with a dump truck, hauling gravel for the township. His obituary was as simple and easygoing as the man himself. "Frank was a graduate of Severy High School. Frank owned and operated Frank Bills Trucking for 50 years. Frank also farmed and raised cattle. He was a member of the Cattleman's Association, and KCC. Frank enjoyed going to the coffee shop first thing every morning to visit with all of his friends. He enjoyed driving around; working his cattle and watching his crops grow."

The government insists on street signs in the middle of nowhere, ridiculous this suburban intrusion on intentionally remote places.

He quietly built his trucking business, United States Department of Transportation Number 130386, to thirty-three tractors and fifty-one trailers, employing forty-one drivers, who took their loads of dry bulk, general freight and livestock more than four million miles down the road in 2013. And even more quietly still, this unassuming man acquired little parcels of land here and there, putting together by the day of his death more than fifteen thousand acres in Greenwood County, Kansas. His family kept a significant amount of land but sold sixteen individual tracts that brought them $13.5 million. Most of the buyers were from out of state, but some of the land went to local buyers. Just as an old truck driver might have wished.

Land sells out here for reasons far apart from its agricultural prospects. There is just so very, very much urban and corporate interest right now in the ownership of land, almost any land, that notions of familial tradition, rancherly longevity or cultural inheritance seem quaint, silly almost. Land to be leased for hunting and fishing is simply not available; it's taken, thank you.

In the intergenerational passage of pasture ground, the teeth jarring comes typically with the grandkids. Removed for the most part from the history of the grass's use, but aware in no uncertain terms of the land's immediate monetary worth, the heirs of these hills have no problem selling land that some tenant ranching families have cared for across the better part of a century. An aged and involved landowner dies, and the thirty-something inheritors decide that a distant half-section of faceless bluestem seems just like sudden money in the bank. And only the big boys, the really big boys, have their fingers in the air at bidding's end.

A living language necessarily suffers some abuse. Amid the push and shove of daily life in English, words slowly lose some of the oomph with which they arrived. Few words have suffered the belittling endured by the adjective "awesome." Its root noun originally described the emotions appropriate to a direct encounter with God. The Almighty alone might inspire awe. For several centuries in Great Britain and her colonies, only transfigurations of the human form, white bread falling from the sky, and stones rolled without explanation from the doors of tombs deserved the descriptor "awesome."

American teenagers of recent memory have pretty much taken care of that particular interpretation of the word.

Last August, I went to Washington, D.C., looking for something, anything, truly awe-inspiring. On my first-ever visit to our nation's capital, I hoped to rediscover the first meanings of a three-letter word. Lincoln's Second Inaugural Address etched there on the north wall of his memorial came close. So did fifty-some-thousand names on a long, too long, black wall, my old buddy Second Lieutenant John Simmons among them. And then it happened. In the gray morning quiet of the National Cathedral, beneath a nave eighty-three years in the making, the word jumped unasked from my mouth.

But once the surprise of my visceral response to Episcopalian architecture had passed, I quickly realized that the surprise was misplaced, a function of being on vacation maybe, the artificial product of a willful intent to find again a feeling that maybe has been here all along. Sitting in our national house of prayer, I began to remember other Hail Marys, some outdoor Glory Bes. I began to think of how something like awe routinely informs my life on the ranch. Of how—a newborn calf, shined black and silver with licked placenta and struggling so to stand on too long legs—I've crossed myself, looked to an endless sky and said, "Thank you, Sir."

The inspiring and the inspired among us remain a throwback to another time, back when life reduced to a few undeniable facts, and the consequences of a decision showed up sooner rather than later. But a sense of mystery can live on, the occasional miracle can still occur in this hard century, in this faraway place.

I live among cathedral stones of another stripe. I walk on limestone that makes the bluestem strong, and I see that bedrock honesty and genuine love of neighbor inform the best of lives. Encounters with the absolute are a natural and inevitable part of the cowboy way, of a life lived in caring for cattle horseback. As a carryover from an idealized vision of America, the cowboy ought to be well equipped to restore those ideals, to show an inevitably urban populace the collective and individual rewards of a rural ethic.

At least, isn't it awesome to think so?

PART III
LOOKING FORWARD: THE LIFE TO COME

Mitch and Karaline Mayer

Karaline Poovey grew up on a farming and ranching operation 140 years old. The Poovey headquarters stands outside of Oxford, Kansas, a Sumner County small town so law abiding, so clean and wholesome and true that the home page of the municipal website comes with a disclaimer. Read on at your own risk.

> *Oxford is a historic small town located in Sumner County, Kansas on Highway 160. Oxford has been named a TREE CITY USA for over 10 years. The town site sits on the west bank of the Arkansas River. Little Town Square is in the heart of the City and provides a place to sit and enjoy the activities downtown. The Oxford Public Library provides special programs during the year such as the Summer Reading Program, Page Turners Book Club, Books and Babies, Story Time and other fun activities. It is understood that, while the City of Oxford has no indication and reason to believe that there are inaccuracies in the information presented on this website, the City of Oxford makes no representations of any kind, including but not limited to warranties of merchantability or fitness for a particular use. Nor are any such warranties to be implied with respect to the information, data or service furnished herein.*

Mitch and Karaline Mayer, agricultural entrepreneurs.

Now Karaline Mayer, married to Mitch, works as the agricultural-extension agent for Wabaunsee County. Kara M. is as good and right and smart as her hometown's no-nonsense website. Her family raised cattle, and there were always horses about—saddle horses, of course, but Belgians as well, good to have around for pulling mountains in a pinch. There were mules, too. "My granddad had a jack," she says, and in his will, the old gentleman willed a buggy to Karaline, thinking that this young woman would appreciate its significance, as most surely she does.

She knows the significance of marrying a Mayer. Mitch, the two-words-a-minute horseback cowboy, says, "You can always tell a German, but you can't tell him much." In the joke comes the strength of their marriage, the go-it-alone, no-regrets entrepreneurism of their move away from a century and a half's worth of Mayer work and tears on nearby pieces of Kansas.

Mitch and Karaline found each other in the study of animal science at Kansas State University in Manhattan. They dated there, and then, as Karaline says, "I left Mitch for two years," and indeed she did. Study of meat science at the University of Nebraska, a master's degree taken there, and she came on home to him, and they moved into a massive two-story house on the Mayer ranch, and Kara had begun the keeping of a promise to herself, "I will live my life in the Flint Hills."

The house had "character," as she says. "The curtains blew with the windows shut," as her husband says. And then they moved. They moved away from Mitch's family and the inherited way of life waiting there. But, as with all of Carl Folk's great-great-great-great-grandkids, they understood the necessary subdivision of the old family place, more Mayers wanting to come back to the work and the beauty along Millcreek Road just east of Alta Vista.

And so P.J. Mayer, Mitch's brother, still rides the family's pastures down south, and he does so with the ease of horseback observation of the born cowboy. But P.J. has also taken a job in town. No big deal. One does what one needs to support one's family.

His brother has chosen to strike out on a frightening little deal that has brought him south of Paxico, Kansas, to a bermed, beflowered structure far more energy efficient than the windblown house with character back on the ranch. He and Karaline, with a little one due in October, have found a separate peace—she riding off on a twenty-five minute commute ("this road the closest place to God in the entire county") to Alma, the county seat, where she and the other extension agent for the county remain active in two ways: pro and re.

Proactive: 4H first and last and always, educational courses scheduled for reasons both long-term and ad hoc and targeted publications that answer many of the questions.

Reactive: Expert seat-of-the-pants stuff that answers every question through the door, from pest control to the planting of Austrian pine trees, from calf scours to cookie recipes.

Karaline manages the politics of the office as well, the meetings with the county commissioners, the calls from Topeka, and so her hours stretch well beyond the expected forty. With the baby imminent, she will find in her and Mitch's quiet, efficient way the means of dealing with a job off their homeplace. Come next springtime, Karaline Mayer will leave her baby and her cowboy to bring a long day hence the cash money and the health and other benefits that make her county-agentdom worthwhile and workable, the right job for the moment as she and Mitch work toward the dream.

Meanwhile, her man is riding the pastures, looking for the sick ones, waiting to solve any problem, to make life better in any way in his power for these animals in his care. He's preoccupied with the cattle in these pastures, his insistence on looking at them daily, on vouching to himself for their health and growth, their well being no matter the season. He watches for the first signs of hoof rot in a wet last spring. He puts the mineral out in anticipation of the summer's growth spurt, two-plus pounds a day on nothing but this grass and the force of a cowboy's will. He rides among some bred heifers, brought to him with the thought that they would calve in September, and he finds a baby or two in the wet grass, and he adjusts the frequency of his visits to this pasture. He's calving heifers of his own.

They're young—Mitch but thirty, his bride a year younger—and they're starting to put it all together, their own spread, the place that they'll pass to this beautiful child not yet born. It comes in little pieces, three-quarters of section to Mitch's care over here, a section there, two more a long way down this county road, but it's coming together, leasing now, land so far beyond their ability to buy. These two, soon three—however, they're in this Flint Hills deal for the long, long haul.

And this gorgeous land, this bountiful grass, will expect them. No warranties. But then, no real hurry either.

THE BAILEYS

Wayne Bailey was born a cowboy, and as such, he is probably entitled to name his notion of the cowboy's principal skill. Wayne says it's "looking around." He believes that the best cowboys are always observing, almost never asking dumb questions. And when he does wonder why, the born cowboy accepts both the inevitability and the deep, sweet irony implicit in the fundamental question, "What else would I do?"

Wayne has ready answers for the two practical questions the locals most often ask him.

One, the open-cockpit airplane was indeed a necessary cowboy business expense, a useful and highly efficient means of looking around.

Two, he has already enjoyed and lost the one great horse every born cowboy should be entitled to.

The horse, Rascal, proved to be the equine equivalent of everything Wayne Bailey himself wanted to be: ready to work cattle all week and more than ready to haze steers on Saturday night. Rascal gave Wayne seven good years, and then a twisted gut battled first the veterinarian in Eureka, Kansas, and then the learned surgeons at Kansas State University in Manhattan, because not less than everything would be attempted in saving this horse's life.

Wayne Bailey graduated with the last class of Matfield Green High School, where goats have now enrolled.

When it didn't, Wayne cried like a just-weaned calf.

As most certainly he did not when his sternum was extended an inch or so from the inside out, the product of a teenage encounter with a cheap saddle horn. His nose now is quite a little bit more mashed and wayward than the nose he was born with. He has learned to throw a loop with both hands somewhat late in life, after a gray mare beat his right side half to death in the quiet stall on a Sunday afternoon, earlier in which he had won yet another buckle at a ranch rodeo forty miles down the road.

Marcia Stout married Wayne Bailey on November 23, 1968, one week to the day after his return from service as a combat engineer in Vietnam, "the first place I'd ever been that didn't have a rodeo," he says. "There was no courtship," she says. Theirs was a marriage of shared respect earned in the competitions of county fairs, in the sun and dust of patterned horse races: the poles, the barrels, the "rescue race" with a junior-high Wayne waiting behind a barrel and horseback Marcia reeling by, her husband-to-be swinging on behind for a full-out sprint to the finish line. "There was very little love back then," she says again. "We wanted to kill each other." The murder spree ended in that near-fifty-years-gone November.

And the really hard work began.

The eventual lovebirds were born into old Flint Hills ranching families, unspoken rules bred five generations deep, life lessons learned in choir practice Wednesday evenings at the Presbyterian Church in Cottonwood Falls, in watching banger cows leaving the ranch with that hateful "B" brand, going immediately to slaughter. "Profit" a strange and foul-mouthed word in this line of work. Marcia following her dad everywhere back then, Elmore Stout at ninety-two years of age still in charge of TS Herefords and Quarter Horses, Bazaar, Kansas, the ranch begun by Marcia's grandfather, A.E. Titus, MD, an old-timey doc, who in the course of hundreds of horse-and-buggy miles delivered maybe five thousand babies hereabouts. Marcia's brother Stanley was studying at Kansas State University at the start of a regionally legendary auctioneering career, but not before one last bit of instruction from Elmore: "You make damned sure we can understand every word you say."

It has been this way from the "I dos" on.

The wedding dance done, Marcia and Wayne moved into a ten-foot by fifty-foot trailer house, took to riding pastures that Derward Bailey, Wayne's dad, handed down to his son and his son's new wife—the care of pastures that thirty years before, Jess, his own dad, had given him to ride. The payment for six months of watching over some thousands of steers came in October, a single check representing the newlyweds' ostensible income for the entire year, and Bailey household budgeting was suddenly a long-term deal. And so Wayne went off to the oil fields, roughnecking through the winter, a little extra money to carry Marcia and him to spring and the cattle coming again. Wayne dug basements. They took in yearlings in the cold months. They built fences, did daywork where they could find it. "This country will teach you versatility," she says. The Baileys guaranteed the counts and cared for the cattle as if they were their own, and they tried to build the acreages entrusted to them. Wayne taught kids to rodeo, just as Derward had taught him.

Mike Wiggins, old Albert's son, remembers four nights of practice and two nights of competition in the high-school years, he and a dozen other young cowboys back then spending golden hours at the arena Wayne built south of the house, down along the road. "One night we didn't want to quit, and we lined our pickups along the side of the arena, and we bulldogged in the headlights," Mike remembers.

Marcia Bailey of Greenwood County, Kansas, arrived straight out of a gene pool valuing intuition and persistence and no-questions reliability and always-on skills of observation, the key attributes of the cowgirl. Naturally, the neighbors took notice. One, whose ranch lies a few miles south of Wayne and Marcia's spread, says, "If I needed help in catching a wild one, if I needed a good count on a bunch of cattle strung all over a couple of sections, I'd call Marcia Bailey first." Marcia stayed on the ranch, doing a strong man's work, dehorning, calving heifers, holding a hundred newborns down for the cutting on a given day.

In time, the young couple started Bailey Construction. No finish carpenters here, no painters, Bailey Construction interested itself in horsepower, in large loads delivered at high speed, in movement at once explosive, accurate and purposeful. (Some neighbors have referred for years to the entire Bailey operation as the "Power Ranch.") And Marcia in time operating every piece of equipment in the yard, but one truck—usually the only street-legal vehicle in the fleet—always referred to as "Marcia's dump truck," the ten-speed, tandem-axle International in which she hauled both Buck and Wes as babies from a Chase County quarry the seventy miles one way to job sites in Wichita, her toddler sons wrapped in blankets in the cab of the truck, loading river gravel at four o'clock in the morning, way before the cows had to be fed.

When the hauling, cowboying and roughnecking paid enough for gas, Marcia and Wayne went down the road, rodeoing throughout the first fifteen years of their marriage, he up in the bulldogging, she hazing for him. Marcia riding those barrels like unto cash for groceries. "I can't say that we ever made much money from our rodeoing," he admits, "but when I won, we ate steak."

The circuit gone old, the family times packaged in memory books of her own making, Marcia Bailey thinks of the cowboy Elmore. "I grew up in his shadow," she says again of the cussed-tough old man, the patriarch's strength all hers now. Her boys grown, at work on their own ranches, Buck having bought his grandparents' ancestral Matfield Green place, Wes eight miles north of Durham, Kansas, on some old Stout ground, Wes rodeoing still—in the family manner—winning saddle-bronc in last winter's incarnation of the invitation-only, big-arena "Barebacks, Broncs, and Bulls" competition, Wes free to travel to Eugene or Peoria as the schedule demands because Rachell (Mrs. Wes Bailey), in the way of Marcia Stout Bailey and her mother, Doris, and grandmother Jessie, is looking after the cattle back in Kansas. A rodeo man may have to make Cheyenne, but sometimes he does so only because a ranch woman is bucket feeding calves five hundred miles away in a wind-driven barn unaccustomed to a crowd's approving roar.

A ranch woman named Marcia finds herself alone in the middle of an unpopulous country for sixty or seventy days in just the hardest coming of the winter, starting at daybreak, checking fluid levels in the feed truck, loading

In April, cattle flood into the hills, ready for grass that in a good year will put three pounds a day on a steer.

the daily ration of hay and cubes for two hundred cows spread over three pastures, heading out in the January gloom to chop ice eight inches thick on south-siberian ponds, the bale strings frozen in grassed-up glue. And Marcia with the window rolled down and looking—looking for the sickies, trying to catch the problems early, the ancient cowboy wisdom taking hold, "If you look twice at a calf, there's a reason to worry." Marcia listening again, hearing Elmore whisper across the years, "That cough doesn't sound quite right."

Marcia Bailey has fed cattle by herself for the past eight winters because her husband has a way with large diesel engines and their manual controls. Even in high school (Matfield Green, Kansas, 1965, graduating class of four), Wayne was already manhandling bulldozers, the old D7 cables, building dams, clearing brush, cleaning feedlots, developing an affinity for heavy machinery that has taken him to William's Lake, British Columbia; later to Labrador City, Newfoundland; and finally to Salt Lake City, Utah. To make budgetary ends meet, since 1998, Marcia's husband has disappeared each autumn, off to maintain and repair impossibly massive mining equipment.

Amid sensitivities a watchmaker might want, Wayne Bailey and his friends raise a three hundred thousand–pound shovel on patented jacks invented by a cowboy mechanic so that its operating table might be milled to tolerances of eight one-thousandths of an inch, specialized work, obviously, requiring specialized tools and know-how accumulated over several lifetimes spent around heavy machinery. The paychecks match the job description, good money at no time available back in rural, hard-frozen Kansas.

Buck Bailey's great-great-granddad, Colonel George Washington Bailey, came to these hills just after the Civil War, famous in these parts for telling a neighbor who was stitching up a deep, ugly cut in this foot, "Put another stitch there, Albert," pointing to an uncut spot of skin. "It'll look better if you even things out." Born out of such random toughness, Buck has lost two-thirds of the acreage three-quarters of a century in his family's care, and what's a cowboy to do without the grass on which to run his herd? So he goes with his father and his neighbors to Nova Scotia, British Columbia, Arizona and Utah, wherever the mining industry finds itself in need of an oil change. Buck's mom maintains the homeplace and waits for her men to find their way back home.

But guess what—after a fifteen-year hiatus, Bailey Construction is up and running at six thousand revolutions per minute once more. Marcia operates now with a new hip, a replacement that took her out of the saddle for most of last summer, not an especially happy time, but one that she bore with typical good humor: "I had more time to sew." Wayne's bulldogging has left him with reaching shoulders mushed up and sore, a day at the controls of a grappled front-loader full of not much but pain and achievement. But at least he's underfoot, the winter just past looking to be for the first year in memory a connubial proposition on the Power Ranch.

And so here they go again, cutting trees this time around. Grubbing out hedge eighty-some years in the hardening. Ripping through the red cedar like so much overtall grass. Hoping to make the nut, five hundred dollars a day, that waits winters in the mines up north. Hoping to stay home next fall, to cut trees in the slack, to be there feeding cows with Marcia come February, no need to go back to fourteen-hour days in places where the sun shines, maybe, eight. Not on a good day, back home, Elmore gone now—no more sixty-mile trips to check on Dad—and a few hours in the basement with some cowhide.

Marcia Bailey makes purses. She makes pillows and table runners and covers for photo albums. She weaves a delicate tapestry—a cowgirl, smiling, slides away horseback—against chap leather with white stitching and silver studs. An ostrich insert struts all around crinkled calf leather accented with conchos and a horsehair tassel. White brindle tucks next to red calf hide basted all about with red diamond sparkles and a black fringe. Marcia Bailey makes purses for a couple of reasons. One, her handiwork creates a welcome supplemental income to her family's well being. Two, the contemporary products of her mind, eye and hand hearken back to the wellsprings of her cowgirl creativity. That pillow there, this picture frame right here…well, they're just Bazaar, Kansas, 4H projects that don't ever have to end.

Make no mistake: the trees cut, the leather crafts made and sold, they matter. They matter in enduring economic terms because the grass is going. Insidiously. Whole sections disappearing with not ten minutes' warning, pastures the Baileys and the Stouts have managed for seventy years and more, pastures that Derward and Elmore, as young men, cared for, land now lost to an urban, intergenerational predilection for a fast buck.

The plane is no longer a part of Bailey ranch life. Wayne relinquished it after some very productive years of livestock flight operations but, truth be known, after several cowboys' lifetimes of looking around. Wayne flew one last mission, a water-balloon raid on a neighbor replacing a roof, engine off, Bailey on a glide path, silent just above the twenty-mile-per-hour stall speed, ready to bomb with both hands. He came over Main Street in Eureka once with a cockpit full of water-swollen plastic in that J-3 Cub, a plane he used to check pastures that two cowboys couldn't ride in two days, a plane he crash-landed the first day he flew it, in front of a half-dozen Mexican jet pilots who had brought their owners in for a registered Brangus sale south of town. Wayne stepped from the Cub, its fuselage vertical a hundred feet from the runway, and he bowed and he waved his hat to the sprinting, laughing jet jocks. Some of them wanted to buy what was left of that J-3, a plane capable of sustaining an ace undone in his first attempt at leaving this earth.

At the time, the salvaged airplane was not for sale. Unlike old Rascal, a good airplane can be rebuilt. And so Wayne's wife, Wes and Buck's mom, sits with a good and true friend making simple objects of grace and beauty, their handiwork salable and happening in big-city stores in numbers that only the real deal can deliver. With any luck at all, come Christmas, Buck's dad will be right there too, sewing the heavier leathers next to a wife of almost fifty years, likely both of them remembering.

Remembering calves dragged and pregnant heifers helped along and grieving neighbors brought some brisket, thinking back to Jess and Jessie, to Derward and Opal and the golden-throated Stanley. Knowing that the grass around here grows good amid some sympathy and some homegrown science. Thinking how it has come round to this: to the certain assumption between two horseback cowpeople that every last little heartache, every unexceptional joy of two lives well lived has led right here.

Right here to downtown Thrall, Kansas.

THRALL, KANSAS

The Emancipation Proclamation pretty much took care of thralls in America, but Abe Lincoln was dealing only in the small "t" sense of the word. It still exists only on the very best maps of this part of the world, but the Thrall that lies two miles north here has never been an uppercase kind of capital in the world's view of things, not even when its own brief boomtown status put it right there with your Whizbang, Oklahomas in terms of your sudden growth, your lopsided economic importance of a particular industry (in Thrall's case, oil), your fiduciary imbalance between your single daytime industry and various nighttime businesses it spawned and, of course, your fairly sudden disappearance from the face of the earth.

A backfire begins the springtime burning of a pasture just south of Thrall.

There's a sign halfway through the bombed-out storm cellars and the two or three ghost houses with asbestos shingles that constitute downtown Thrall, a sign that asks you please not to fish the tepid water below this rock bridge with its three-inch bluegill because this here is a microbiologically interesting but still very public water supply. My neighbor's cow herd pretty much has the run of both your east and your west as well as your own downtown Thrall, and not once have I seen an old girl within one hundred yards of this particular water supply. I'll tell you what though: the best sunrises, the best sunsets in the whole world originate in Thrall, Kansas.

Noontime's mostly not worth spit.

THE NELSONS

His first name is Tom, but it could just as easily be Ozzie—Harriet's husband, David and Ricky Nelson's dad—because the old fifties family sitcom, *Ozzie and Harriett*, could be to all outward appearances Tom Nelson's life.

Tom grew up in a small, picturesque Kansas town where his father farmed and his mother taught school. His grandmother lived with his family and kept a diary, a sentence or two every day about the weather, about an especially good meal or a visit from a friend, and those simple details accumulated to a happy life lived where expectations didn't really matter. Tom married his high-school sweetheart after earning a degree in animal science. He worked for a time in backgrounding stocker cattle before finding his way back to Olsburg, the little largely Swedish community where he grew up. He has purchased the old home place from his mother and lives there now at a busy, but simultaneously easy, pace that comes straight out of Ozzie Nelson's idyllic fatherhood of early television.

Tom's great-grandfather moved onto the farm in 1904, beginning an unbroken tenure of Nelsons at home north of Olsburg. Again this year, Tom has purposely planted four acres of his corn crop late so that the stalks will be tall and green come October, when he will cut a maze through it as part of the Pumpkin Patch with hayrack rides behind Tom's team of Percherons, blacks, the draft horses that he bought on a long-thought whim seven years ago—2007, the year of the first maze, that first fall in which all his own children helped in the preparation of the maze.

The horses are well broke, not high-spirited enough for the athletic pulling competitions, but just perfect for parades and hauling kids around. In the Lawrence (Kansas) Parade, with only horse-drawn entrants allowed, Tom's

Donica and Tom Nelson with their pet Percherons.

team pulled a 1904 fire-department steamer, whose fires drove the pumps that filled the hoses a century ago. Fitting, altogether right and good, that Tom should be enjoying these horses, since he and his brother Dick were both named after draft horses, the boys born just before his dad turned to tractors to till this Pottawatomie County soil.

Tom works at a financial institution that also sells eggs and milk, but which, "as a matter of principle," does not use business cards for its officers.

The details of this life built around church and family rapidly approach stereotype—they're that idyllic.

Initially, Donica Buell wanted no part of it. "My family moved to little Olsburg from Kingman, Arizona, when I was a teenager," Donica says. "My schools had obviously been much larger and more diverse, and then suddenly I find myself in a high-school senior class of sixteen. The whole experience was very difficult." By graduation, she was more than acclimated. By her wedding day, she was telling Tom that he need not bother considering any marital future involving a big city. Their children have been the direct beneficiaries of their parents' decision.

Nelson daughter, Erin, took a degree in biology from Bethany College in Lindsborg, it also too all-American for words. She met Curtis Gutsch there, from Lincolnville, Kansas, where his family farmed. She has married and come back home to open a small restaurant and grocery store.

Son Brandon, now married and living in Lawrence, is studying chiropractic, after which he and wife, Chandry, hope to live in some rural place.

Son Byron is working a part-time job to support his study at Brown-Mackie in Salina; he will soon become a veterinary technician, using every day the science supporting a love of animals he learned north of town.

Byron's fifth-grade class was once asked to write about the best advice they'd ever been given in their young lives. Byron's answer came short and strong. "Go outside," he wrote. The wise advisor toward outdoor living: his father, Tom Nelson.

Grown and gone, the Nelson kids have indelible memories of sloppy joes every Saturday night, with who knows how many of their friends over to eat—of sleeping well and happily in horse trailers at junior livestock shows and of their own private, outside kid place, where they'd go with their stuffed animals and later their backpacks stuffed with Mom-made goodness, that hideout where adult reality suspends, where all things seem possible.

As indeed, Tom and Donica Nelson proved once when, with but $200 to their name and no job waiting out ahead, they decided that you really can go home again.

THE MAYERS

In the sixth decade of the nineteenth century, even farmers and stonemasons living a quiet, agricultural life in Petersdorf, Germany, could not escape the rampant militarism of Otto von Bismarck, who threatened to suck every man of fighting age into his armies. Or, conversely, into defense against his armies. And so Carl and Frederecka Falk and their children, Carl II and Anna, took off. Took way off.

Onto a ship for a sixty-three-day voyage to America that brought them here just eleven months before Fort Sumter and the beginning of our own Civil War.

The Falks pioneered it out to Kansas, the Union's newest state by the time of their arrival, and they settled down along Rock Creek a few miles north and east of Alta Vista. The Falks began the creation of a new life along the creek, and they did so in specific, Teutonic order, the patriarch Carl making himself known among other Wabaunsee County settlers in, first,

The gun ports on the north wall of the Mayer barn waited for marauding Indians, who never did arrive.

the building of Zion Lutheran church; second, the formation of Templin School (named after another town near Petersdorf back in Bavaria); third, the construction of a fort for protection against marauders off the nearby Kaw Reservation. The nonmilitaristic Carl soon built gun ports into the foot-thick stone walls of his new barn, but ongoing conflict with his Native American neighbors never did develop—a most fortunate deal indeed since a few other difficulties did arrive in the form of frequent prairie fires, raging like war itself across the deep grass of a fertile prairie, and of grasshoppers that arrived in sun-blocking swarms that sounded like a hailstorm, hordes that ate the wool from live sheep and the bark from trees, armies whose carcasses made rails so slippery that locomotives could not maintain traction.

Then, as reported in Matt Thomson's *Early History of Wabaunsee County, Kansas with Stories of Pioneer Days and Glimpses of Our Western Border*, "Mr. Herman Fink had come over from Germany and was boarding with Mr. Carl Falk of Templin. Smallpox broke out on the ship on which Mr. Fink came across the ocean but he escaped the disease. But the germs evidently secreted themselves in his clothes-chest, for several weeks after his arrival he gave his clothes an airing and then the smallpox germs began making trouble. Mr. Falk's family was the first to be taken down." In fact, Carl had gone with a wagon on the long, multiday trip to Kansas City to procure provisions when the rash and the backaches, the fatigue and the high, high fever set upon his Henry, born after Emelia and Augusta, before Maria and Wilhelmine, in this new place of fire and grasshoppers, before the rains came at last and hope became possible. Alone on the farm, Frederecka wailed into winds that simply would not stop.

Carl II and his son, Herman, continued to fight the weather and the market into the next century, taking big Texas steers off the railhead at Volland from the Chicago, Rock Island and Pacific Railroad there miles from Alma, the county seat, Volland with a telegraph office and a general store of Falk–extended family ownership. By 1910, Volland's population had grown to twenty-six, and up and down the creek had come a hard-headed prosperity in farming and ranching in keeping with many of the ways of the old country. The Falk name morphed then into Mayer, Willard Mayer keeping the ranch's familial operations alive and traditional—only once and for a short time did a cattle herd bear the Mayer brand. For all of the ranch's years, job satisfaction has come in the well being and security of other people's cattle, and Don and Hal—Willard's sons, the sixth generation of cowmen in this family—wouldn't change much about their business or their way of life.

Consider: a special ceremony at the 2011 Kansas State Fair was convened to honor the Mayer ranch on its sesquicentennial, a prestigious affair that Kansas governor Sam Brownback attended, but which Hal and Don Mayer did not. They were busy back home feeding cattle. Slicking up some steers for delivery to buyers who always know what they have in cattle purchased from the ranch there on Rock Creek: animals ready to go, to perform as advertised in the local sale ring, in a private treaty or through the ranch's brokerage, Superior Livestock Auctions.

The Mayers always look for light calves, and they have covered the country in pursuit of the cattle most likely to prosper on the mixed diets that their native grass and their cultivation make possible in a starting yard just outside Don's back door. These cattle are watched—watched carefully and looked after with the practiced eyes of men who know land and cattle and crops. Always, always the cost of gain uppermost in their minds, and they've searched from Wyoming to West Virginia to find the calves that will fatten best on their custom feeding. Right now, lightweights from Pennsylvania, many of them with black hides, are proving to respond best in the Mayers' pens on their miraculous grass, both deeded and leased. Their operations stretch across five thousand acres in five counties of prime Flint Hills country, the farthest pasture thirty-five miles from headquarters. Five hundred of those acres are given over to crop production, to the silage that constitutes such a large and important part of the calves' ration in the yards.

They're volunteer firemen, both of them, and the Mayer brothers have just come through an especially long burn season, ranchers picking their times, their spots, to strike the match at just the best possible time—for them—to knock back the weeds, to give the grass the boost that only those few seconds of flame can bring.

The Mayers know what they have in this bluestem, the Indian grass and the grama, and they guard it carefully, protecting the resource that has sustained their family for seven generations.

If the kids can make it back.

Hal's boys, Travis and Blake, help when they're needed. "There just isn't a place for them right now," their dad says with resignation that's not quite a smile. Don's son P.J. looks after the south pastures, while another son, Dana, pitches in too on those days when an entire family of experienced hands and strong backs needs to be on the job at hand.

If the kids can make it back, the question that hangs over the day-to-day, the summer-to-summer. If the kids can make it back.

There comes some uncertainty in the brothers' faces, some hesitation in their voices: "The boys want to carry on our family's way of life, but we're not there yet," says Hal Mayer. His brother chimes in, "Maybe we'll have to retire early. I don't know yet how we're going to make the transition. Fact is, I don't know yet if we can make the transition while Hal and I are still alive." Don Mayer looks at you, his hands the size of bear paws, and you believe him.

The Lundbergs

In the flood of 1993, the waters of Tuttle Creek Reservoir came within seventy-five yards of the carefully landscaped and groomed front yard of Karen and Steven Lundberg. "For a while, we had a beachfront home," says Steven, with the calm detachment of a man justly angered at his family's treatment at the hands of the United States Corps of Engineers. In the easements demanded by the corps, the family had sold them, at eminent domain, primo farm ground for $150 an acre, such bottomland as now sells routinely at $3,000 an acre. The 1993 corn and wheat crops lost to the mud and the slop, Steven could think back to another year, to 1961, when his father was forced off his farm for the construction of the reservoir.

The Great Flood of 1951 roared through this country, inundating downtown Manhattan. The response, both predictable and logical, called for the construction of a flood-control project as might protect the city and other communities downriver. The farmers and ranchers who saw the flooding of their own land as the inevitable result of Tuttle Creek's construction fought back with organized opposition in the sort of argument that honestly does pit brother against brother. "Let's quit this dam foolishness," their battle cry, but the upriver landowners ultimately lost their fight, and in 1962, ten Kansas towns slid away under the rising waters of a reservoir that not everybody wanted.

The Corps of Engineers, they treat this land like dirt.

In 1993, when the eighteen Tuttle spillway gates were opened for the first time, sixty thousand cubic feet of water blasted through every second, producing a roar audible a half-mile away. Twenty-some miles north, the flood still surged toward Steven and Karen Lundberg's front door, and they sat there and watched the coming edge of the killer water, and they did as they always do. They accepted what they could not change, and with their children, they set about the continuation of the only existence they might ever want.

Steven remembers living along the river with a low-water bridge over to the house. He remembers even more the swinging bridge over which they walked when the river rose, a shaking and hesitant stepping across the bridge and then a ride on a wagon behind the tractor the mile and a half back to the house.

"I've never worked a day in my life," Steven says from the experience of his sixty years, a man who loves his livelihood in a place that will serve until the call of the gathering angel. "My dad was born north of Randolph" (the only sunken town to rebuild after the submersion of the dam's completion), "and he moved four times to, off and back to this place." The homeplace. Where Angie, Corey, Trevor and Nathan were born.

Steven and Karen raised their children in 4H. They slept with their animals at the state fair. They cooked every meal on the fairgrounds. "We raised the hamburger here and grilled it there," as Corey says.

Now Nathan lives over in Clay Center, where his grandson Chase had a sixth birthday yesterday, but he's pushing his luck, and he's calling Grandma's

Steven and Karen Lundberg, salt of the earth.

house to talk about presents with both his uncles there too. Chase's grandpa smiles and says he'll call the boy back.

Angie has taken her K-State degree in animal science out to Chinook, Montana, where she works with an embryo transplant service. Trevor and his wife, Maggie, rent farmground from an elderly neighbor, land that happens to fall on each side of the homeplace. Corey works for a rancher by Onaga, Kansas, helping to care for eight hundred cows and a couple thousand yearlings. He runs thirty cows of his own on a pasture down the road from the house where he grew up. He's horseback every day. Karen helps out at the livestock auction in Marysville on sale days. She keeps the barn's books as well.

Forty years ago, the Lundbergs started their cow herd with fifty heifers the day after the patriarch dropped a kitchen chair on his bare toe, the same day the truck hauling the starters was ticketed by the Kansas Department of Transportation. From these inauspicious beginnings, the herd bearing the ancestral LK brand has grown, its health and safety assured by a family of Swedes who practice thrift as naturally as breathing, Steve and Karen's husbandry quiet and strong as a new five-wire fence.

The Lundbergs count their blessings. They've had to sell down but never sell out, their cow herd intact since the day of the sore toe and the speeding ticket. "We're fortunate to have more rainfall in this part of the state," Steven suggests. "We're not going to run out of water up here, and we'll always have roughage for our cattle. With our row crops we can maintain a balance in our income year to year; we're not relying on money from the cow herd." The family stockpiles hay and feed, beyond the bales off the alfalfa acreage expected to be fed in a coming winter, beyond the thousand tons of corn silage, beyond the wheat for grazing in the cold months.

But Steven knows that, for all of his planning and all he has learned in the day-to-day of running his family's farm, he doesn't have it all figured out, that the ever more efficient use of resources comes in observation and response, in the difference between looking and seeing. He and Karen know that, no matter how hard they work, "there's just not enough here" to pass along to all of their children. And so a Lundberg of the next generation, maybe two, will come back. That much is certain. A child of theirs will care for this ground. And in some strange and unforeseen likelihood, perhaps all four of them will find a way to share again this family ground, this remote and silent place.

Unlike any other topography in Kansas, these steep hills, these valleys and meadows, this deep black soil has given the Lundbergs a family table that will not soon be empty. As on this particular June Tuesday, Karen has cooked ahead for her children coming to visit, Steven swathing alfalfa until the rains blew in.

Then he piddled in the shop until time for a supper that comes before dark only because of the weather.

JAN AND FRANK LYONS

On December 23, 2003, in the state of Washington, the United States Department of Agriculture made a preliminary diagnosis of bovine spongiform encephalopathy (BSE) in one nonambulatory, severely disabled dairy animal. That single downer cow set off again international hysteria over mad cow disease, the fatal neurodegenerative disorder that CNN so lovingly immortalized with halting black-and-white videography of a Canadian cow staggering to her knees. Over and over, the clip of that poor mama aired on American television, and the world took note: Japan immediately halted all beef imports from the United States, to be followed by full or partial restrictions on American beef products by sixty-four other countries. Export of our beef declined the following year, 2004, by 978,000 metric tons.

Presiding in large part over the domestic cattle industry's response to this public relations manure storm was a quiet, quietly accomplished woman from rural Riley County, Kansas: Ms. Jan Lyons, president of the National Cattlemen's Beef Association. Jan woke morning after morning in Washington, D.C., and Atlanta and New York City to address the mad-cow frenzy in news conferences full of questions both pertinent and impossibly ignorant, in press releases waiting to counter the day's big-media take on everything that might be wrong with hamburger in America. "As we took on that whole issue," she remembers, "we quickly learned that targeted messages full of factual, scientific information delivered in a calm, thoughtful, forthright and transparent way were the best way to effectively communicate the ongoing safety of our product." This nation's beef industry survived the onslaughts common to her years of service, and Jan came on home then, back to her herd and the bloodlines building there. She still speaks of the "pride and gratification I felt watching the family come together, taking on more and more of the daily operation of the ranch when I was forced to be away so much."

Her voice softens, speaking fundamental notions of contentment, with gratitude for the goodness of her life as she describes the new medical practice of Dr. Frank Lyons, the man she met at The Ohio State University, before coming to Kansas to Fort Riley, the post where Frank's military obligation called him to first practice medicine; where at Kansas State University, Jan earned a master's degree in counseling; where six years later and the girls just toddlers, she and Frank discovered out there by McDowell Creek, a few miles straight south of Manhattan, a place to make it perfect.

Frank became a broadly respected radiologist serving small Kansas towns with a big city sort of medical expertise, a subspecialty in which, like cattle ranching, there's something new to be learned every twenty-four hours or so. Across a long career in town, he helped out on the big days on the ranch, horseback with his grandkids. And now, after retiring from his radiology practice, he has found the beginning excitement of a young resident physician in his work with regenerative surgery, a revolutionary process called adipose stem cell therapy. Working in a new partnership, Kansas Regenerative Medicine Center in Manhattan, Dr. Lyons is pioneering a procedure in which the patient's own stem cells, drawn from fatty tissue, can lead to healing of ailments ranging from damaged ligaments to asthma, from painful joints to strokes. Jan herself has taken advantage of her husband's work to find relief in a damaged knee.

The Lyons ranch raises Angus cattle with studied emphasis on traits that determine the profitability of the customer, a heavy responsibility. And so the bulls in the annual early-spring sale—last year's sale the ranch's twenty-fifth—represent a careful, predictable balance of fertility, calving ease and carcass value. The cow herd consists of productive females from strong cow families with proven genetics and mothering ability. Jan describes her herd as "honest and straightforward," cattle recognized in Kansas and surrounding states for their primo Angus genetics, genetics all family-selected, the foundation females chosen long ago from the major-reputation breeders in the region. All animals are DNA tested for higher accuracies on such traits as calving ease, growth, marbling and ribeye area—all selected to greater profitability for customers. Daughter Amy and her husband, Karl Langvardt, part-owners of the Lyons ranch, work with her day to day on the north ranges of the ranch, while living among Lyons pastures south a ways, near Alta Vista, Kansas.

Jan has always been in agriculture. Her farmer father passed away five years ago, and her brother, Bill, has taken over the family place back in

Columbiana County, Ohio. "My dad ran cattle on the farm where I grew up," she says. "As a little girl I was always more interested in following him around than staying in the house with my mom." Determined that her daughters would enjoy the outdoor joys, the quiet lessons of the ranching life that had been her own girlhood, she brought them along as her leadership activities in the industry grew from local volunteering with 4H beef programs and property-rights groups, on to become president of the Angus association and then a representative to the Purebred Council and president of the Kansas Livestock Association in its 1994 centennial year, a position that involved her with the National Cattlemen's Beef Association where more and more committee work at last led to her accepting the association's chair in 2004.

The Lyons Angus Ranch is a strong, clean spread with native grass that grows thick above the limestone soil, a hilled and watery place with a century-old, big-porched house that the Lyons family has made beautiful, lived in with grandchildren now almost all grown, ready to make big decisions about the direction of their lives. The ranch remains a place very far away from a world where the ignorant winds of zealotry blow office buildings down, where hatred might fly blind in stolen planes to spray death from the sky. But Jan Lyons never could say no to a good agricultural cause, and so she sat knowledgeably among United States senators and generals from the Joint Chiefs of Staff and agribusiness executives as a member of a task force addressing this nation's response to bioterrorism. As the Homeland Security folks made their decision about the location of a research and development facility, she worked all the while, as she always has, to ensure that rational, direct, honest and straightforward thinking prevailed. And so the National Bio and Agro-Defense Facility is coming out of the ground about six miles north of Jan Lyons's kitchen. The new facility will look for and then develop measures to fight biological threats from terrorists, the fiends who might use transmittable diseases to attack either human or livestock populations.

"The presence of the center is good for the community," she says, "with its scientific prestige and several hundred jobs there, jobs bringing some high salaries. We need to be studying the diseases on the center's agenda, but still it gives me pause. I see, however, an even greater danger from the Environmental Protection Agency." The closest of the Lyons pastures lie within the facility's epicenter, should a catastrophic release of toxins occur.

At the same time, she finds her ranch and her livelihood under attack from other agencies of the federal government, the Environmental

Jan Lyons, visionary.

Protection Agency most of all. "I was up in a pasture at the top of the hills just this morning," she says, "where these old buffalo wallows retain water, and different flora develops there. Theoretically, those wallows—private property—could be regulated. It's madness. We must have legislation to stop these proposed EPA regulations on water."

In the face of bureaucracies she's encountered up close and personally, she says, "We earn no salaries in agriculture. We're left with costs and prices. If American agriculture loses control of our costs, people are going to go hungry. Farmers and ranchers are perfectly capable of regulating ourselves. We understand what's necessary to produce food for the world while creating opportunities for our young people to live this lifestyle. The regulators may perhaps mean well, but they're misinformed. They don't understand how food is produced. We work here everyday as caretakers."

She looks ahead, she and Frank, realists both, and they ask, "Is there a fit for these grandchildren back here? Can we help them somehow to make a living here? Can we grow some part of the business to make room for another grandkid or two?" Land stands, of course, as the constraining factor. Right now, with the overall ranch operation running smoothly, there are profits for reinvestment, for new equipment and the acquisition of such grass as might come available. "We've built the brand of this ranch," its matriarch says. "As long as we do the right thing for our customers, as long as we maintain the integrity of the brand, we'll be fine. My dad always told me that I could do anything I wanted. I have no doubt about the abilities of my children and grandchildren, and Frank and I are working to give them such opportunities as we can."

For the moment, a troubled and unregenerative world seems so very far away. And blessed words are these—"integrity," "grandchildren" and "opportunity"—most especially when they come from a person so completely genuine, so at peace with herself and her surroundings that love of family, love of her work, love of her cattle and her country radiate exactly like this perfect morning's prairie sunshine.

The Blythes

Debbie Lyons-Blythe has just changed the name of her blog from "Life on a Kansas Cattle Ranch" to "Kids, Cows, and Grass," as she says, her three passions. In the announcement of the change, she wrote about her children and her cattle with a sense of nurture as big as the solemn sky of Morris County, Kansas. And then she turned to the hills: "All grassland because the pioneers found it was too rocky to farm. There is plenty of good farmground around us, but the bulk of the land is in the same grass that the buffalo ate centuries ago. It is still here because of people like me, taking care of it, removing the invasive plants and caring for it so that it will still be a fertile land for my kids and grandkids."

Love is work, ranchers know. Hard, sometimes dangerous work that speaks of love of family, of the land that supports them. "Three of our five children have told us they want to come back to the ranch," Debbie says, "and Duane and I are working hard to make their return possible."

Duane is an investment banker, and his skills in financial and estate planning have proven central to the family's thoughts about the future. When five children arrive in four and a half years, the need for financial planning asserts itself with some inevitability in the forecast. Here came Meghan, now twenty-three; Allie twenty-one; Trenton, twenty; and the twins, Eric and Tyler, now freshmen in the Delta Upsilon house at K-State. "When we had nothing, we began to save. We opened five different 529s [tax-favorable college savings plans]. The minute we got pregnant, we started putting money away."

Nothing glib in the "we" in Debbie's description, the Blythes' marriage a true and lasting partnership in which the two decided that Duane would earn a living in town, that she would resign as Morris County extension agent, that a stay-at-home ranch-mom would be the only way to go. This particular late spring day, Debbie picked up Meghan at kindergarten, the other four in car seats, and off they went to put out mineral. The Blythe kids' dad had just put in a new crossing for the creek, and in the unsettled rock, the Blythe kids' mom found herself stuck. She looked into the back seat to see Trenton there with his cowboy boots on the wrong feet, with no socks. So, in an act of supreme motherly love, she took off her own socks, made them somehow work on Trent's toddler feet, and off they all went—mom carrying the twins—on a two-mile trek across rough country to a neighbor's house, where they arrived sunburned and hungry—but safe. The neighbors handed out snacks all around, pulled the truck out of the muck and waved good-bye as Debbie and her kids went back out to finish the distribution of the mineral that, in beef cattle, supports normal bodily maintenance, growth and reproduction. The major minerals subsumed in the cowboy singular "mineral" include calcium, phosphorus, magnesium, potassium, sodium, chlorine and sulfur, as Duane and Debbie's kids, all grown up now, will gladly discuss with any interested party.

Early on, those youngsters came to understand the meaning of taking hold. Like their dad. At fourteen years of age, his father's funeral two days past, Duane Blythe climbed on the tractor, taking over the farm, the huge brand on the barn a reminder to a serious, seriously tested teenager that he was his family's only hope for this land homesteaded by his great-great-grandfather.

The urgency of Duane's years ahead of the plow has eased now, but the responsibilities of family, each to each, remain. From an early age, the youngsters have been given a voice in the ranch's decision making, not often a vote, but always a voice. As the kids' knowledge grew and their experience deepened and broadened, their opinions carried more weight. "It's not enough to just tell a kid to go rake hay," their mom says. "It's important that they learn why we rake hay at a given time, in given weather conditions. They need to see the effects of changes in the ration. I know that all of my children have woke up some mornings and groaned to themselves that they really didn't want to deal with cows today," Debbie says, "but I know what they've gained over the years from their responsibilities on the ranch." For all of their obvious success in raising a strong, vibrant and happy set of children, the elder Blythes remain so very humble. "We must never think we're not going to make some mistakes along the way, but our basic insistence on respect has guided our parenting—respect for self, respect for parents and grandparents, respect for siblings, respect for adults, respect for the animals in our care, for the land that supports us." And then Debbie Blythe laughs. She laughs so hard that she shakes as she thinks of her squabbling children forced to sit holding hands with their cantankerous others. If Tyler and Meghan found themselves engaged in some loud disagreement over a book or a toy, the two would be sat sternly down and allowed to continue their blood feud while holding hands. While working even, little fingers wrapped around each other's.

The operation is self-sufficient. A neighbor comes to help with the feeding in the winter months, but otherwise all the labor on the place is familial as on February 24, 2013, when the worst storm of the season blew into north-central Kansas. All the artificially inseminated calves were due on February 24, although fifty cows had calved early. Tyler and Eric were still living at home, in their last semester at White City High. The storm canceled some, but not all, Friday classes in Manhattan, and Meghan made it home to help.

When Monday classes were canceled, Allie and Trenton, the other two Blythe K-Staters, came home to compose a second shift of sorts. By Sunday evening, the entire herd had calved safely, and one cold, very tired family slogged back to the house for a long winter's nap.

"It's a great time to be a cow-calf producer. We're looking at ways we can expand, more with the farming probably," Debbie says. The Blythes have wintered about three hundred cows in recent years, although in 2010, four hundred cows watched for twin boys in the front seat of a feed truck. And then in the spring, after her mother's sale, Debbie will sell about fifty registered Angus bulls at private treaty, an exchange she obviously enjoys. Debbie Lyons-Blythe speaks with an easy joy about her family and her life in this beautiful place, but an extra measure of pride comes into her voice when she talks of her perfect record, of the fact that never has a potential buyer looked at her offerings and failed to buy a bull. "But then, I've held back the very best animals from our calf crop, the bulls who should be bulls."

For all the kids, the opportunity stands: come back home to take over the cattle operation and perhaps diversify the possibilities for profit. But first they have to go away, to confront the wonderful unknown. "Duane and I have tried to give them the very best rural upbringing we could. We love small towns, we really do, but we want each of the kids to see what's out there, what might be waiting for them."

And so Meghan, the oldest, works as a compliance officer in Colorado for JBS, the international meat company. Allie is studying hotel and restaurant management, interning this summer in a hotel at Glacier National Park. Trent will be a junior in wildlife and outdoor enterprise management, a new K-State program teaching the mechanics of establishing and operating a hunting lodge, an entrepreneurial program that borrows from Trent's sister's major while emphasizing biology, conservation and training in firearms. Talk around the table at the Blythe household and up south of Manhattan at Grandma Lyons's place turns often to new possibilities for the entire family. "What's good for cattle is also good for bird populations," Debbie says. "Trent wants to guide in Alaska, and he will. But who knows? Maybe someday he'll think about coming home to see what we might build here." Eric and Tyler will study animal science together, wearing, as always and forever, the silver and purple of Kansas State University.

In 2012, Debbie was named Farm Mom of the Year, her children having nominated her months previous. For Mother's Day 2012, her kids built and installed a purple martin house.

As the days of their lives together report the red-letter days set among the work and the weather, the blog, with its new name, will give new and continued expression of one family's respect for each other, for their cattle and for their land.

Finding there an enduring, such a formidable, joy.

Annie Brown

For almost thirty years, I have lived among cowboys, men whose one and only desire in this life is to ride the range, men who cry like love-struck girls at the death of a good horse and who stand dry eyed in the rain at a best friend's funeral, men whose acceptance I sought, whose approval might come my way if I kept dumb questions to a minimum and never, not once, pretended to know more than I did.

Annie's family made it all possible, the cowboy way bred four generations deep in them, my 110-pound blonde wife a top hand for sure, doing things right, shortcuts of any sort anathema to her strict and certain conscience. Work brittle, afraid of not much beyond rattlers in the springtime, soothing of hurts human and otherwise, she galloped through my life on the ranch with the moral authority of the born cowgirl she was.

They say each of us carries the cells that will eventually be the death of us. I walk around this morning nurturing the murderous exponents of my own undoing. Maybe cancer really does lie in the arroyos of all human metabolism. Maybe it menaces a kindergarten sweetheart on a Western Auto tricycle as surely as it does her eighty-year-old grandfather, the sun-loving Copenhagen addict who bought the trike on his pension from the uranium mine. For Annie, the killer came with insidious intent, with a viciousness that began to seem like special treatment. Three times, we believed she had wrestled this rare cancer to a draw, had fought off its want for her cervix. Told at diagnosis that the cancer typically appears in women twice her age, as one of the lesser of their medical problems, I knew that surely her silent strength, the purity of her thoughts, her will to see our teenage daughter in a wedding dress would bring her through, no matter what the medical oddsmakers might say.

And so she began the haul: surgery first, in the ruined hours of an endless Saturday, she lay in the laying open of her front side, the navel and down thereabouts. But the killer tissue was taken and some lymph nodes too, and I shot off my fat mouth. "Annie Brown beat cancer," I said, blind from denial in a deal jinxed from the get-go.

Annie Brown, cowgirl.

Annie was a creature of autumn. Born on the last day of August, she turned to harvest, to nurturing, to warming a winter place. Frugal, tightfisted with our money, she understood the value of things. She bought the best clothing, on sale, took care of it and wore it with the easy verve that won my heart away. We'd agree each fall that it would be Thanksgiving before we turned on the furnace. Any cold snaps beforehand—well, we had sweaters and the fireplace and chili and early bedtimes. A friend stopped in Target once, watching Annie touch and snoop in the housewares aisle, and he knew too. "She's nesting," he said.

A thoughtful, inventive giver of gifts, she loved her themes. One Christmas, all her gifts—from the gaiters to the wool shirt to the guitar picks in my stocking—were red. We traded anniversaries. One September 17 would be Annie's responsibility, the next would be mine. She took me fly-fishing in Montana and New Mexico, the latter a resort owned by the Apaches, people after her own heart.

She gave me this horse on our tenth wedding anniversary. Jumpy, stumble footed, by her own admission, not a handsome horse, Annie Brown decided that Clyde would be my mount. He bit Mike Collinge's horse square on the ass, without provocation, our first time out with the locals. Walked right up and, before any sort of how-de-do, chomped down on that horse's beam. Someone asked, "Ain't that the Clyde horse?" And then, "Too bad about those little girls." Quicksilver fast, he had run barrels until his accidents with those young women became too much for his owners to bear, speed not much when kids are being flung toward rodeo dirt.

With me, he tripped, but he did not tip over. He stumbled, again and again, but never did he fall. Until that Sunday afternoon when all hell headed east and old Clyde jumped out from under me, and off we were going in pursuit of the breaking heifers. Past Harold Garner, venerable University of Missouri professor in equine studies of the more esoteric sort. Past good old Norman Geiger. Down we went, this horse and I, as a direct result of his fuel-dragster speed, his intuitive notion that we should be there rather than here. The hole in the terrace too big even for a far surer horse to miss, his tonnage rolled over me, the saddle horn missing by an inch the bone at my left knee, ribs broken and a shoulder torn, a concussion unknown but underway.

He jumped back erect, standing there, waiting for me to come along. He stood, and he waited. I climbed back on, as the unspoken dictum said, and the burn ensued and my ribs could not support the weight of my head and shoulders. I drooped in the saddle, and Mike Seeley, Annie's brother, took me in his pickup back up the hill where she waited to help and to heal one more time.

Well.

Twice the disease came back, each recurrence mysterious and unprecedented to the gynecological oncologists who treated her, even to those at the MD Anderson Cancer Center in Houston, where a Bulgarian physician of soft and earnest voice asked what he might do for her. "Please prolong my life," she said, and he gave back some clinical horrors with not much hope. So Annie came home to die.

We had already brought the goals closer, had shortened the landmarks of our hope. No longer thinking of a daughter's bridal gown. No more graduation from college. Not even from high school now.

On this certain day, we had gone to town for a trim of her hair, growing back a bit after the cessation of the chemo that had failed to save her. On Lake Road, she told me to buy a new truck immediately, so that "people won't talk about you whooping all our money away after I'm gone." We passed the funeral home, and she said, "Let's stop and pick out a casket for me."

When I protested, she said, "But surely you've thought about my dying."

"I was thinking about Hilltop."

"Oh, I'd like that."

Hilltop, last used in 1949, a hateful woman buried at the cemetery's northernmost edge, her casketed feet facing away from the neighbors whom she despised in life and wanted little to do with in death. Hilltop, blue-stemmed burial ground for soldiers from the Grand Army of the Republic and for clustered babies, taken in the diphtheria epidemic of 1911, the disease finding its way from ranch to ranch in this remote hill country, abetting the deaths in childbirth, often mother and stillborn baby taken within hours of each other's passing. Hilltop Cemetery, where Leonard Booth told me that South Janesville Township policy required the purchase of four plots minimum, and "John, that'll be twenty-eight dollars." Hilltop, five miles as the crow flies from the house she had designed over ten years of reading *Southern Living* magazine.

She died at three thirty on a Monday morning, her life spilling out in a little blood at the nose and mouth, in a release of the bowel obstruction that had tortured her since Friday. I sat in the chair next to our bed of nineteen years and watched her slip away.

Father Leo Kerschen, who loved her from first sight, sang "Home on the Range" from the pulpit. The funeral procession stretched for nine miles, some cars just leaving Sacred Heart Church back in town as the first vehicles parked in the pastures adjacent to Hilltop, Suzie Hawthorne's horses stampeding along the way, never having seen such a sight.

Oh, she would have liked that.

She cried, to my knowledge, three times in the years the cancer worked its worst. Her tears came unwelcome at diagnosis, then again at the doctors' recommendation of hospice. And finally, a week before she died, I walked into the house from feeding the cattle to find her shaking on the couch. Her dry mouth puckered, Annie's eyes red in the hurt of the disease's gnaw, she

said to me, "I can't remember how many cows we have. I can't remember," and she cried some more.

Little saint. Little love of mine.

She lay there gloried, bald and white, her love for this sweet old world consumed in the altogether of trying to draw another breath, a standoff of minute-to-minute proportions. I brought our cows up to the house pasture, so that she might see them from our bed, their calves running and bucking across our grass, its billion swallowed hoofbeats echoing in her tiny, silent ears.

And just like that, there they went, those black babies and my Annie, riding off with all the answers, hard, into the wind.

A blizzard is expressing itself toward Oklahoma, the snow coming level against the bent grass. The wind icepicks my face on the first step out of the truck. A chapped smile lights the skies, and the ranchhouse with its two by eight framing hangs tough against the blow. The solitude, the cold, the crazed thump of the wind crowd in, and the lonesome is so easily located, a welcome sort of separation. I have toughened some to the feelings imposed by these distances and their inability to reach a conclusion. My friend Hugh Greer, who paints these hills, always includes a structure of some sort in his work: "Otherwise, I wouldn't know where to stop." Hugh's right. You must watch this country for a long, long time before you attempt an understanding. You dink around, you dabble, you doubt, you don't get confirmed.

A while ago, I went looking for rocks for the patio in an excuse to work outside, to find some solid, if small, achievement in the blur of a blue norther. I loaded eighty-pound chunks of limestone on the bed of the feed truck. I cranked the heater on the drive home, with the windows down. I saw again the big buck with a rack glorious and angry even from the road. I waved at Latham Wiggins, Albert's grandson, on his way up to check heifers in the Martindale, Latham almost done at Oklahoma State, ready for whatever comes next, Latham who on the first day I met him was swinging on a rope with a towel around his neck. "Call me Powerman," he said.

I see old Calvin Bewley walking with his rake along Bachelor Creek. And Kathryn Jackson there on her porch and Melba in her little shop. I feel Albert Pickell's poke in my chest. I hear Wayno overhead in that bombplane of his, flying all night to some last-chance rodeo. I remember Annie's grandpa, lifting his head from the pillow on which he would soon die, telling us to, please, go make some memories. I think of all my neighbors in their houses, their goodness making romantic the murderous elements in wait on the other side of a shaking door, and the honor of it all giddies me.

The ranch is empty now. Hawk, responsible for three of my broken ribs in the horseback years, died last week. My sister-in-law walked around the corner of the barn, startled him upright. Old Hawk looked once around, and that damned outlaw fell over dead.

The cold outside but this hushing warmth everywhere near, I rub the bottoms of my feet together, and I feel therein the orbiting of the spheres. Well-lit. Musical in the squeeze of the moment. And just before I fall asleep, the easy retreat into the sanctity, the happiness of the all alone, I think of what Willa Cather said, "This land wants only to preserve its mournfulness. We have no real right to leave a mark here."

The real cowboys don't.

ABOUT THE AUTHOR

John Brown has ghostwritten six biographies and corporate histories. Last year, The History Press published *Wichita State Baseball Comes Back*, a five-year history of the resurgence of the baseball program at the university. *People of the Flint Hills: Bluestem Prairie Portraits* comes as his most recent work from a freelance career in marketing, advertising and magazine editorial during which he has completed almost five thousand writing assignments.

He has taught writing at Kansas State University, at Wichita Collegiate School, at Butler County Community College and in the California Correctional System, where inmates seeking to leave their gang lives behind use writing as a tool in their work toward eventual parole.

He lives with his wife, Lee Ann, in Wichita and on their ranch in the Kansas Flint Hills.

Visit us at
www.historypress.net

....

This title is also available as an e-book

www.ingramcontent.com/pod-product-compliance
Lightning Source LLC
LaVergne TN
LVHW010950100826
845153LV00002B/186

* 9 7 8 1 5 4 0 2 1 1 8 4 2 *